BIRDS IN THE BUSH

Bradford Torrey

HAWK PRESS

Published by

Hawk Press
4836/24, Ansari Road, Daryaganj
New Delhi – 110 002
Phones : 9643330713, +91-11-23278618, +91-11-35676207
E-mail : thehawkpress@gmail.com
www.thehawkpress.com

ISBN : 978-93-92322-84-6

Contents

ON BOSTON COMMON.

Nuns fret not at their convent's narrow room;
And hermits are contented with their cells;
And students with their pensive citadels:
Maids at the wheel, the weaver at his loom,
Sit blithe and happy; bees that soar for bloom,
High as the highest Peak of Furness-fells,
Will murmur by the hour in foxglove bells:
In truth, the prison unto which we doom
Ourselves, no prison is: and hence for me,
In sundry moods 't was pastime to be bound
Within the Sonnet's scanty plot of ground;
Pleased if some Souls (for such there needs must be)
Who have felt the weight of too much liberty,
Should find brief solace there, as I have found.

— Wordsworth.

ON BOSTON COMMON

Our Common and Garden are not an ideal field of operations for the student of birds. No doubt they are rather straitened and public. Other things being equal, a modest ornithologist would prefer a place where he could stand still and look up without becoming himself a gazing-stock. But "it is not in man that walketh to direct his steps;" and if we are appointed to take our daily exercise in a city park, we shall very likely find its narrow limits not destitute of some partial compensations. This, at least, may be depended upon,—our disappointments will be on the right side of the account; we shall see more than we have anticipated rather than less, and so our pleasures will, as it were, come to us double. I recall, for example, the heightened interest with which I beheld my first Boston cat-bird; standing on the back of one of the seats in the

Garden, steadying himself with oscillations of his tail,—a conveniently long balance-pole,—while he peepedcuriously down into a geranium bed, within the leafy seclusion of which he presently disappeared. He was nothing but a cat-bird; if I had seen him in the country I should have passed him by without a second glance; but here, at the base of the Everett statue, he looked, somehow, like a bird of another feather. Since then, it is true, I have learned that his occasional presence with us in the season of the semi-annual migration is not a matter for astonishment. At that time, however, I was happily more ignorant; and therefore, as I say, my pleasure was twofold,—the pleasure, that is, of the bird's society and of the surprise.

There are plenty of people, I am aware, who assert that there are no longer any native birds in our city grounds,—or, at the most, only a few robins. Formerly things were different, they have heard, but now the abominable English sparrows monopolize every nook and corner. These wise persons speak with an air of positiveness, and doubtless ought to know whereof they affirm. Hath not a Bostonian eyes? And doth he not cross the Common every day? But it is proverbially hard to prove a negative; and some of us, with no thought of being cynical, have ceased to put unqualified trust in other people's eyesight,—especially since we have found our own to fall a little short of absolute infallibility. My own vision, by the way, is reasonably good, if I may say so; at any rate I am not stone-blind. Yet here have I been perambulating the Public Garden for an indefinite period, without seeing the first trace of a field-mouse or a shrew. I should have been in excellent company had I begun long ago to maintain that no such animals exist within our precincts. But the other day a butcher-bird made us a flying call, and almost the first thing he did was to catch one of these same furry dainties and spit it upon a thorn, where anon I found him devouring it. I would not appear to boast; but really, when I saw what Collurio had done, it did not so much as occur to me to quarrel with him because he had discovered in half an hour what I had overlooked for ten years. On the contrary I hastened to pay him a heart-felt compliment upon his indisputable sagacity and keenness as a natural historian;—a measure of magnanimity easily enough afforded, since however the shrike might excel me at one point, there could be no question on the whole of my immeasurable superiority. And I cherish the hope that my fellow townsmen, who, as they insist, never themselves see any birds whatever in the Garden and Common (their attention being taken up with matters more important), may be disposed to exercise a similar forbearance toward me, when I modestly profess that within the last seven or eight years I have watched there some thousands of specimens, representing not far from seventy species.

Of course the principal part of all the birds to be found in such a place are transient visitors merely. In the long spring and autumn journeys it will all the time be happening that more or less of the travelers alight here for rest and refreshment. Now it is only a straggler or two; now a considerable flock of some one species; and now a miscellaneous collection of perhaps a dozen sorts.

One of the first things to strike the observer is the uniformity with which such pilgrims arrive during the night. He goes his rounds late in the afternoon, and there is, no sign of anything unusual; but the next morning the grounds are populous,—thrushes, finches, warblers, and what not. And as they come in the dark, so also do they go away again. With rare exceptions you may follow them up never so closely, and they will do nothing more than fly from tree to tree, or out of one clump of shrubbery into another. Once in a great while, under some special provocation, they threaten a longer flight; but on getting high enough to see the unbroken array of roofs, on every side they speedily grow confused, and after a few shift ings of their course dive hurriedly into the nearest tree. It was a mistake their stopping here in the first place; but once here, there is nothing for it save to put up with the discomforts of the situation till after sunset. Then, please heaven, they will be off, praying never to find themselves again in such a Babel.

That most of our smaller birds migrate by night is by this time too well established to need corroboration; but if the student wishes to assure himself of the fact at first hand, he may easily do it by one or two seasons' observations in our Common,—or, I suppose, in any like inclosure. And if he be blest with an ornithologically educated ear, he may still further confirm his faith by standing on Beacon Hill in the evening—as I myself have often done—and listening to the chips of warblers, or the tseeps of sparrows, as these little wanderers, hour after hour, pass through the darkness over the city. Why the birds follow this plan, what advantages they gain or what perils they avoid by making their flight nocturnal, is a question with which our inquisitive friend will perhaps find greater difficulty. I should be glad, for one, to hear his explanation.

As a rule, our visitors tarry with us for two or three days; at least I have noticed that to be true in many cases where their numbers, or size, or rarity made it possible to be reasonably certain when the arrival and departure took place; and in so very limited a field it is of course comparatively easy to keep track of the same individual during his stay, and, so to speak, become acquainted with him. I remember with interest several such acquaintanceships.

One of these was with a yellow-bellied woodpecker, the first I had ever seen. He made his appearance one morning in October, along with a company of chickadees and other birds, and at once took up his quarters on a maple-tree near the Ether monument. I watched his movements for some time, and at noon, happening to be in the same place again, found him still there. And there he remained four days. I went to look at him several times daily, and almost always found him either on the maple or on a tulip tree a few yards distant. Without question the sweetness of maple sap was known to Sphyropicus varius long before our human ancestors discovered it, and this particular bird, to judge from his actions, must have been a genuine connoisseur; at all events he seemed to recognize our Boston tree as of a sort not to be met with every day, although to my less critical sense it was nothing but an ordinary specimen of the common Acer dasycarpum. He was extremely industrious, as is the custom of his family, and paid no attention to the children playing about, or to the men who sat under his tree, with the back of their seat resting against the trunk. As for the children's noise, he likely enough enjoyed it; for he is a noisy fellow himself and famous as a drummer. An aged clergyman in Washington told me—in accents half pathetic, half revengeful—that at a certain time of the year he could scarcely read his Bible on Sunday mornings, because of the racket which this woodpecker made hammering on the tin roof overhead.

Another of my acquaintances was of a very different type, a female Maryland yellow-throat. This lovely creature, a most exquisite, dainty bit of bird flesh, was in the Garden all by herself on the 6th of October, when the great majority of her relatives must have been already well on their way toward the sunny South. She appeared to be perfectly contented, and allowed me to watch her closely, only scolding mildly now and then when I became too inquisitive. How I did admire her bravery and peace of mind; feeding so quietly, with that long, lonesome journey before her, and the cold weather coming on! No wonder the Great Teacher pointed his lesson of trust with the injunction, "Behold the fowls of the air."

A passenger even worse belated than this warbler was a chipping sparrow that I found hopping about the edge of the Beacon Street Mall on the 6th of December, seven or eight weeks after all chippers were supposed to be south of Mason and Dixon's line. Some accident had detained him doubtless; but he showed no signs of worry or haste, as I walked round him, scrutinizing every feather, lest he should be some tree sparrow traveling in disguise.

There is not much to attract birds to the Common in the winter, since we offer them neither evergreens for shelter nor weed patches for a granary. I said to one of the gardeners that I thought it a pity, on this account, that some of the plants, especially the zinnias and marigolds, were not left to go to seed. A little untidiness, in so good a cause, could hardly be taken amiss by even the most fastidious taxpayer. He replied that it would be of no use; we hadn't any birds now, and we shouldn't have any so long as the English sparrows were here to drive them away. But it would be of use, notwithstanding; and certainly it would afford a pleasure to many people to see flocks of goldfinches, red-poll linnets, tree sparrows, and possibly of the beautiful snow buntings, feeding in the Garden in midwinter.

Even as things are, however, the cold season is sure to bring us a few butcher-birds. These come on business, and are now welcomed as public benefactors, though formerly our sparrow-loving municipal authorities thought it their duty to shoot them. They travel singly, as a rule, and sometimes the same bird will be here for several weeks together. Then you will have no trouble about finding here and there in the hawthorn trees pleasing evidences of his activity and address. Collurio is brought up to be in love with his work. In his Mother Goose it is written,—

Fe, fi, fo, farrow!

I smell the blood of an English sparrow;

and however long he may live, he never forgets his early training. His days, as the poet says, are "bound each to each by natural piety." Happy lot! wherein duty and conscience go ever hand in hand; for whose possessor

"Love is an unerring light,

And joy its own security."

In appearance the shrike resembles the mocking-bird. Indeed, a policeman whom I found staring at one would have it that he was a mocking-bird. "Don't you see he is? And he's been singing, too." I had nothing to say against the singing, since the shrike will often twitter by the half hour in the very coldest weather. But further discussion concerning the bird's identity was soon rendered needless; for, while we were talking, along came a sparrow, and dropped carelessly into a hawthorn bush, right under the shrike's perch. The latter was all attention instantly, and, after waiting till the sparrow had moved a little out of the thick of the branches, down he pounced. He missed his aim, or the sparrow was too quick for him, and although he made a second swoop, and followed that by a hot chase, he speedily came back without his prey. This little exertion, however, seemed to have provoked his appetite; for, instead of resuming his coffee-tree perch, he went into the hawthorn, and began to feed upon the carcass of a bird which, it seemed, he had previously laid up in store. He was soon frightened off for a few moments by the approach of a third man, and the policeman improved the opportunity to visit the bush and bring away his breakfast. When the fellow returned and found his table empty, he did not manifest the slightest disappointment (the shrike never does; he is a fatalist, I think); but in order to see what he would do, the policeman tossed the body to him. It lodged on one of the outer twigs, and immediately the shrike came for it; at the same time spreading his beautifully bordered tail and screaming loudly. Whether these demonstrations were intended to express delight, or anger, or contempt, I could not judge; but he seized the body, carried it back to its old place, drove it again upon the thorn, and proceeded to devour it more voraciously than ever, scattering the feathers about in a lively way as he tore it to pieces. The third man, who had never before seen such a thing, stepped up within reach of the bush, and eyed the performance at his leisure, the shrike not deigning to mind him in the least. A few mornings later the same bird gave me another and more amusing exhibition of his nonchalance. He was singing from the top of our one small larch-tree, and I had stopped near the bridge to look and listen, when a milkman entered at the Commonwealth Avenue gate, both hands full of cans, and, without noticing the shrike, walked straight under the tree. Just then, however, he heard the notes overhead, and, looking up, saw the bird. As if not knowing what to make of the creature's assurance, he stared at him for a moment, and then, putting down his load, he seized the trunk with both hands, and gave it a good shake. But the bird only took a fresh hold; and when the man let go, and stepped back to look up, there he sat, to all appearance as unconcerned as if nothing had happened. Not to be so easily beaten, the man grasped the trunk again, and shook it harder than before; and this time Collurio seemed to think the joke had been carried far enough, for he took wing, and flew to another part of the Garden. The bravado of the butcher-bird is great, but it is not unlimited. I saw him, one day, shuffling along a branch in a very nervous, unshrikely fashion, and was at a loss to account for his unusual demeanor till I caught sight of a low-flying hawk sweeping over the tree. Every creature, no matter how brave, has some other creature to be afraid of; otherwise, how would the world get on?

The advent of spring is usually announced during the first week of March, sometimes by the robins, sometimes by the bluebirds. The latter, it should be remarked, are an exception to the rule that our spring and autumn callers arrive and depart in the night. My impression is that their migrations are ordinarily accomplished by daylight. At all events I have often seen them enter the Common, alight for a few minutes, and then start off again; while I have never known them to settle down for a visit of two or three days, in the manner of most other species. This last peculiarity may be owing to the fact that the European sparrows treat them with even more than their customary measure of incivility, till the poor wayfarers have literally no rest for the soles of their feet. They breed by choice in just such miniature meeting-houses as our city fathers have provided so plentifully for their foreign protégés; and probably the latter, being aware of this, feel it necessary to discourage at the outset any idea which these blue-coated American interlopers may have begun to entertain of settling in Boston for the summer.

The robins may be said to be abundant with us for more than half the year; but they are especially numerous for a month or two early in the season. I have counted more than thirty feeding at once in the lower half of the parade ground, and at nightfall have seen forty at roost in one tree, with half as many more in the tree adjoining. They grow extremely noisy about sunset, filling the air with songs, cackles, and screams, till even the most stolid citizen pauses a moment to look up at the authors of so much clamor.

By the middle of March the song sparrows begin to appear, and for a month after this they furnish delightful music daily. I have heard them caroling with all cheerfulness in the midst of a driving snow-storm. The dear little optimists! They never doubt that the sun is on their side. Of necessity they go elsewhere to find nests for themselves, where they may lay their young; for they build on the ground, and a lawn which is mowed every two or three days would be quite out of the question.

At the best, a public park is not a favorable spot in which to study bird music. Species that spend the summer here, like the robin, the warbling vireo, the red-eyed vireo, the chipper, the goldfinch, and the Baltimore oriole, of course sing freely; but the much larger number which merely drop in upon us by the way are busy feeding during their brief sojourn, and besides are kept in a state of greater or less excitement by the frequent approach of passers-by. Nevertheless, I once heard a bobolink sing in our Garden (the only one I ever saw there), and once a brown thrush, although neither was sufficiently at home to do himself justice. The "Peabody" song of the white-throated sparrows is to be heard occasionally during both migrations. It is the more welcome in such a place, because, to my ears at least, it is one of the wildest of all bird notes; it is among the last to be heard at night in the White Mountain woods, as well as one of the last to die away beneath you as you climb the higher peaks. On the Crawford bridle path, for instance, I remember that the song of this bird and that of the gray-cheeked thrush[1] were heard all along the ridge from Mount Clinton to Mount

---

1. My identification of Turdus Aliciæ was based entirely upon the song, and so, of course, had no final scientific value. It was confirmed a few weeks later, however, by Mr. William Brewster, who took specimens. (See Bulletin of the Nuttall Ornithological Club, January, 1883, p. 12.) Prior to this the species was not known to breed in New England.

Washington. The finest bird concert I ever attended in Boston was given on Monument Hill by a great chorus of fox-colored sparrows, one morning in April. A high wind had been blowing during the night, and the moment I entered the Common I discovered that there had been an extraordinary arrival of birds, of various species. The parade ground was full of snow-birds, while the hill was covered with fox-sparrows,—hundreds of them, I thought, and many of them in full song. It was a royal concert, but the audience, I am sorry to say, was small. It is unfortunate, in some aspects of the case, that birds have never learned that a matinée ought to begin at two o'clock in the afternoon.

These sparrows please me by their lordly treatment of their European cousins. One in particular, who was holding his ground against three of the Britishers, moved me almost to the point of giving him three cheers.

Of late a few crow blackbirds have taken to building their nests in one corner of our domain; and they attract at least their full share of attention, as they strut about the lawns in their glossy clerical suits. One of the gardeners tells me that they sometimes kill the sparrows. I hope they do. The crow blackbird's attempts at song are ludicrous in the extreme, as every note is cracked, and is accompanied by a ridiculous caudal gesture. But he is ranked among the oscines, and seems to know it; and, after all, it is only the common fault of singers not to be able to detect their own want of tunefulness.

I was once crossing the Common, in the middle of the day, when I was suddenly arrested by the call of a cuckoo. At the same instant two men passed me, and I heard one say to the other, "Hear that cuckoo! Do you know what it means? No? Well, I know what it means: it means that it's going to rain." It did rain, although not for a number of days, I believe. But probably the cuckoo has adopted the modern method of predicting the weather some time in advance. Not very long afterwards I again heard this same note on the Common; but it was several years before I was able to put the cuckoo into my Boston list, as a bird actually seen. Indeed it is not so very easy to see him anywhere; for he makes a practice of robbing the nests of smaller birds, and is always skulking about from one tree to another, as though he were afraid of being discovered, as no doubt he is. What Wordsworth wrote of the European species (allowance being made for a proper degree of poetic license) is equally applicable to ours:—

"No bird, but an invisible thing,

A voice, a mystery."

When I did finally get a sight of the fellow it was on this wise. As I entered the Garden, one morning in September, a goldfinch was calling so persistently and with such anxious emphasis from the large sophora tree that I turned my steps that way to ascertain what could be the trouble. I took the voice for a young bird's, but found instead a male adult, who was twitching his tail nervously and scolding phee-phee, phee-phee, at a black-billed cuckoo perched near at hand, in his usual sneaking attitude. The goldfinch called and called, till my patience was nearly spent. (Small birds know better than to attack a big one so long as the latter is at rest.) Then, at last, the cuckoo started off, the finch after him, and a few minutes later I saw the same flight and chase repeated. Several other goldfinches were flying about in the neighborhood, but only this one was in the least excited. Doubt less he had special reasons of his own for dreading the presence of this cowardly foe.

One of our regular visitors twice a year is the brown creeper. He is so small and silent, and withal his color is so like that of the bark to which he clings, that I suspect he is seldom noticed even by persons who pass within a few feet of him. But he is not too small to be hectored by the sparrows, and I have before now been amused at the encounter. The sparrow catches sight of the creeper, and at once bears down upon him, when the creeper darts to the other side of the tree, and alights again a little further up. The sparrow is after him; but, as he comes dashing round the trunk, he always seems to expect to find the creeper perched upon some twig, as any other bird would be, and it is only after a little reconnoitring that he again discovers him clinging to the vertical bole. Then he makes another onset with a similar result; and these manoeœuvres are repeated, till the creeper becomes disgusted, and takes to another tree.

The olive-backed thrushes and the hermits may be looked for every spring and autumn, and I have known forty or fifty of the former to be present at once. The hermits most often travel singly or in pairs, though a small flock is not so very uncommon. Both species preserve absolute silence while here; I have watched hundreds of them, without hearing so much as an alarm note. They are far from being pugnacious, but their sense of personal dignity is large, and once in a while, when the sparrows pester them beyond endurance, they assume the offensive with much spirit. There are none of our feathered guests whom I am gladder to see; the sight of them inevitably fills me with remembrances of happy vacation seasons among the hills of New Hampshire. If only they would sing on the Common as they do in those northern woods! The whole city would come out to hear them.

During every migration large numbers of warblers visit us. I have noted the golden-crowned thrush, the small-billed water-thrush, the black-and-white creeper, the Maryland yellow-throat, the blue yellow-back, the black-throated green, the black-throated blue, the yellow-rump, the summer yellow-bird, the black-poll, the Canada flycatcher, and the redstart. No doubt the list is far from complete, as, of course, I have not used either glass or gun; and without one or other of these aids the observer must be content to let many of these small, tree-top-haunting birds pass unidentified. The two kinglets give us a call occasionally, and in the late summer and early autumn the humming-birds spend several weeks about our flower-beds.

It would be hard for the latter to find a more agreeable stopping-place in the whole course of their southward journey. What could they ask better than beds of tuberoses, Japanese lilies, Nicotiana (against the use of which they manifest not the slightest scruple), petunias, and the like? Having in mind the Duke of Argyll's assertion that "no bird can ever fly backwards,"[2] I have more than once watched these humming-birds at their work on purpose to see whether they would respect the noble Scotchman's dictum. I am compelled to report that they appeared never to have heard of his theory. At any rate they very plainly did fly tail foremost; and that not only in dropping from a blossom,—in which case the seeming flight might have been, as the duke maintains, an optical illusion merely,—but even while backing out of the flower-tube in an upward direction. They are commendably catholic in their tastes. I saw one exploring the disk of a sunflower, in company with a splendid monarch butterfly. Possibly he knew that the sunflower was just then in fashion. Only a few minutes earlier the same bird—or another like him—had chased an English sparrow out of the

2. The Reign of Law, p. 140

Garden, across Ar lington Street, and up to the very roof of a House, to the great delight of at least one patriotic Yankee. At another time I saw one of these tiny beauties making his morning toilet in a very pretty fashion, leaning forward, and brushing first one cheek and then the other against the wet rose leaf on which he was perched.

The only swallows on my list are the barn swallows and the white-breasted. The former, as they go hawking about the crowded streets, must often send the thoughts of rich city merchants back to the big barns of their grandfathers, far off in out-of-the-way country places. Of course we have the chimney swifts, also (near relatives of the humming-birds!), but they are not swallows.

Speaking of the swallows, I am reminded of a hawk that came to Boston, one morning, fully determined not to go away without a taste of the famous imported sparrows. It is nothing unusual for hawks to be seen flying over the city, but I had never before known one actually to make the Public Garden his hunting-ground. This bird perched for a while on the Arlington Street fence, within a few feet of a passing carriage; next he was on the ground, peering into a bed of rhododendrons; then for a long time he sat still in a tree, while numbers of men walked back and forth underneath; between whiles he sailed about, on the watch for his prey. On one of these last occasions a little company of swallows came along, and one of them immediately went out of his way to swoop down upon the hawk, and deal him a dab. Then, as he rejoined his companions, I heard him give a little chuckle, as though he said, "There! did you see me peck at him? You don't think I am afraid of such a fellow as that, do you?" To speak in Thoreau's manner, I rejoiced in the incident as a fresh illustration of the ascendency of spirit over matter.

One is always glad to find a familiar bird playing a new rôle, and especially in such a spot as the Common, where, at the best, one can hope to see so very little. It may be assumed, therefore, that I felt peculiarly grateful to a white-bellied nuthatch, when I discovered him bopping about on the ground—on Monument Hill; a piece of humility such as I had never before detected any nuthatch in the practice of. Indeed, this fellow looked so unlike himself, moving briskly through the grass with long, awkward leaps, that at first sight I failed to recognize him. He was occupied with turning over the dry leaves, one after another,—hunting for cocoons, or things of that sort, I suppose. Twice he found what he was in search of; but instead of handling the leaf on the ground, he flew with it to the trunk of an elm, wedged it into a crevice of the bark, and proceeded to hammer it sharply with his beak. Great is the power of habit! Strange—is it not?—that any bird should find it easiest to do such work while clinging to a perpendicular surface! Yes; but how does it look to a dog, I wonder, that men can walk better on their hind legs than on all fours? Everything is a miracle from somebody's point of view. The sparrows were inclined to make game of my obliging little performer; but he would have none of their insolence, and repelled every approach in dashing style. In exactly three weeks from this time, and on the same hillside, I came upon another nuthatch similarly employed; but before this one had turned up a leaf to his mind, the sparrows became literally too many for him, and he took flight,—to my no small disappointment.

It would be unfair not to name others of my city guests, even though I have nothing in particular to record concerning them. The Wilson thrush and the red-bellied nuthatch I have seen once or twice each. The chewink is more constant in his visits, as is also the golden-winged woodpecker. Our familiar little downy woodpecker, on the other hand, has thus far kept out of my catalogue. No other bird's absence has surprised me so much; and it is the more remarkable because the comparatively rare yellow-bellied species is to be met with nearly every season. Cedar-birds show themselves irregularly. One March morning, when the ground was covered with snow, a flock of perhaps a hundred collected in one of the taller maples in the Garden, till the tree looked from a distance like an autumn hickory, its leafless branches still thickly dotted with nuts. Four days afterward, what seemed to be the same company made their appearance in the Common. Of the flycatchers, I have noted the kingbird, the least flycatcher, and the phœbe. The two former stay to breed. Twice in the fall I have found a kingfisher about the Frog Pond. Once the fellow sprung his watchman's rattle. He was perhaps my most unexpected caller, and for a minute or so I was not entirely sure whether indeed I was in Boston or not. The blue jay and the crow know too much to be caught in such a place, although one may often enough see the latter passing overhead. Every now and then, in the traveling season, a stray sandpiper or two will be observed teetering round the edge of the Common and Garden ponds; and one day, when the latter was drained, I saw quite a flock of some one of the smaller species feeding over its bottom. Very picturesque they were, feeding and flying in close order. Besides these must be mentioned the yellow-throated vireo, the bay-winged bunting, the swamp sparrow, the field sparrow, the purple finch, the red-poll linnet, the savanna sparrow, the tree sparrow, the night-hawk (whose celebrated tumbling trick may often be witnessed by evening strollers in the Garden), the woodcock (I found the body of one which had evidently met its death against the electric wire), and among the best of all, the chickadees, who sometimes make the whole autumn cheerful with their presence, but about whom I say nothing here because I have said so much elsewhere.

Of fugitive cage-birds, I recall only five—all in the Garden. One of these, feeding tamely in the path, I suspected for an English robin but he was not in full plumage, and my conjecture may have been incorrect. Another was a diminutive finch, dressed in a suit of red, blue, and green. He sat in a bush, saying No, no! to a feline admirer who was making love to him earnestly. The others were a mocking-bird, a cardinal grosbeak, and a paroquet. The mocking-bird and the grosbeak might possibly have been wild, had the question been one of latitude simply, but their demeanor satisfied me to the contrary. The former's awkward attempt at alighting on the tip of a fence-picket seemed evidence enough that he had not been long at large. The paroquet was a splendid creature, with a brilliant orange throat darkly spotted. He flew from tree to tree, chattering gayly, and had a really pretty song. Evidently he was in the best of spirits, notwithstanding the rather obtrusive attentions of a crowd of house sparrows, who appeared to look upon such a wearer of the green as badly out of place in this new England of theirs. But for all his vivacity, I feared he would not be long in coming to grief. If he escaped other perils, the cold weather must soon overtake him, for it was now the middle of September, and his last state would be worse than his first. He had better have kept his cage; unless, indeed, he was one of the nobler spirits that prefer death to slavery.

Of all the birds thus far named, very few seemed to attract the attention of anybody except myself. But there remains one other, whom I have reserved for the last, not because he was in himself the noblest or the most interesting (though he was perhaps the biggest), but because, unlike the rest, he did succeed in winning the notice of the multitude. In fact, my one owl, to speak theatrically, made a decided hit; for a single afternoon he may be said to have been famous,—or at all events notorious, if any old-fashioned reader be disposed to insist upon this all but obsolete distinction. His triumph, such as it was, had already begun when I first discovered him, for he was then perched well up in an elm, while a mob of perhaps forty men and boys were pelting him with sticks and stones. Even in the dim light of a cloudy November afternoon he seemed quite bewildered and helpless, making no attempt to escape, although the missiles were flying past him on all sides. The most he did was to shift his perch when he was hit, which, to be sure, happened pretty often. Once he was struck so hard that he came tumbling toward the ground, and I began to think it was all over with him; but when about half-way down he recovered himself, and by dint of painful flappings succeeded in alighting just out of the reach of the crowd. At once there were loud cries: "Don't kill him! Don't kill him!" and while the scamps were debating what to do next, he regained his breath, and flew up into the tree again, as high as before. Then the stoning began anew. For my part I pitied the fellow sincerely, and wished him well out of the hands of his tormentors; but I found myself laughing with the rest to see him turn his head and stare, with his big, vacant eyes, after a stone which had just whizzed by his ear. Everybody that came along stopped for a few minutes to witness the sport, and Beacon Street filled up with carriages till it looked as if some holiday procession were halted in front of the State House. I left the crowd still at their work, and must do them the justice to say that some of them were excellent marksmen. An old negro, who stood near me, was bewailing the law against shooting; else, he said, he would go home and get his gun. He described, with appropriate gestures, how very easily he could fetch the bird down. Perhaps he afterwards plucked up courage to violate the statute. At any rate the next morning's newspapers reported that an owl had been shot, the day before, on the Common. Poor bird of wisdom! His sudden popularity proved to be the death of him. Like many of loftier name he found it true,—

"The path of glory leads but to the grave."

BIRD-SONGS.

Canst thou imagine where those spirits live
Which make such delicate music in the woods?

— Shelley.

BIRD-SONGS.

Why do birds sing? Has their music a meaning, or is it all a matter of blind impulse? Some bright morning in March, as you go out-of-doors, you are greeted by the notes of the first robin. Perched in a leafless tree, there he sits, facing the sun like a genuine fire-worshiper, and singing as though he would pour out his very soul. What is he thinking about? What spirit possesses him?

It is easy to ask questions until the simplest matter comes to seem, what at bottom it really is, a thing altogether mysterious; but if our robin could understand us, he would, likely enough, reply:—

"Why do you talk in this way, as if it were something requiring explanation that a bird should sing? You seem to have forgotten that everybody sings, or almost everybody. Think of the insects,—the bees and the crickets and the locusts, to say nothing of your intimate friends, the mosquitoes! Think, too, of the frogs and the hylas! If these cold-blooded, low-lived creatures, after sleeping all winter in the mud,[3] are free to make so much use of their voices, surely a bird of the air may sing his unobtrusive song without being cross-examined concerning the purpose of it. Why do the mice sing, and the monkeys, and the woodchucks? Indeed, sir,—if one may be so bold,—why do you sing, yourself?"

This matter-of-fact Darwinism need not frighten us. It will do us no harm to remember, now and then, "the hole of the pit whence we

---

3. There is no Historic-Genealogical Society among the birds, and the robin is not aware that his own remote ancestors were reptiles. If he were, he would hardly speak so disrespectfully of these batrachians.

were digged;" and besides, as far as any relationship between us and the birds is concerned, it is doubtful whether we are the party to complain.

But avoiding "genealogies and contentions," and taking up the question with which we began, we may safely say that birds sing, sometimes to gratify an innate love for sweet sounds; sometimes to win a mate, or to tell their love to a mate already won; sometimes as practice, with a view to self-improvement; and sometimes for no better reason than the poet's,—"I do but sing because I must." In general, they sing for joy; and their joy, of course, has various causes.

For one thing, they are very sensitive to the weather. With them, as with us, sunlight and a genial warmth go to produce serenity. A bright summer-like day, late in October, or even in November, will set the smaller birds to singing, and the grouse to drumming. I heard a robin venturing a little song on the 25th of last December; but that, for aught I know, was a Christmas carol. No matter what the season, you will not hear a great deal of bird music during a high wind; and if you are caught in the woods by a sudden shower in May or June, and are not too much taken up with thoughts of your own condition, you will hardly fail to notice the instant silence which falls upon the woods with the rain. Birds, however, are more or less inconsistent (that is, a part of their likeness to us), and sometimes sing most freely when the sky is overcast.

But their highest joys are by no means dependent upon the moods of the weather. A comfortable state of mind is not to be contemned, but beings who are capable of deep and passionate affection recognize a difference between comfort and ecstasy. And the peculiar glory of birds is just here, in the all-consuming fervor of their love. It would be commonplace to call them models of conjugal and parental faithfulness. With a few exceptions (and these, it is a pleasure to add, not singers), the very least of them is literally faithful unto death. Here and there, in the notes of some collector, we are told of a difficulty he has had in securing a coveted specimen: the tiny creature, whose mate had been already "collected," would persist in hovering so closely about the invader's head that it was impossible to shoot him without spoiling him for the cabinet by blowing him to pieces!

Need there be any mystery about the singing of such a lover? Is it surprising if at times he is so enraptured that he can no longer sit tamely on the branch, but must dart into the air, and go circling round and round, caroling as he flies?

So far as song is the voice of emotion, it will of necessity vary with the emotion; and every one who has ears must have heard once in a while bird music of quite unusual fervor. For example, I have often seen the least flycatcher (a very unromantic-looking body, surely) when he was almost beside himself; flying in a circle, and repeating breathlessly his emphatic chebec. And once I found a wood pewee in a somewhat similar mood. He was more quiet than the least flycatcher; but he too sang on the wing, and I have never heard notes which seemed more expressive of happiness. Many of them were entirely new and strange, although the familiar pewee was introduced among the rest. As I listened, I felt it to be an occasion for thankfulness that the delighted creature had never studied anatomy, and did not know that the structure of his throat made it improper for him to sing. In this connection, also, I recall a cardinal grosbeak, whom I heard several years ago, on the bank of the Potomac River. An old soldier had taken me to visit the Great Falls, and as we were clambering over the rocks this grosbeak began to sing; and soon, without any hint from me, and without knowing who the invisible musician was, my companion remarked upon the uncommon beauty of the song. The cardinal is always a great singer, having a voice which, as European writers say, is almost equal to the nightingale's; but in this case the more stirring, martial quality of the strain had given place to an exquisite mellowness, as if it were, what I have no doubt it was, a song of love.

Every kind of bird has notes of its own, so that a thoroughly practiced ear would be able to discriminate the different species with nearly as much certainty as Professor Baird would feel after an examination of the anatomy and plumage. Still this strong specific resemblance is far from being a dead uniformity. Aside from the fact, already mentioned, that the characteristic strain is sometimes given with extraordinary sweetness and emphasis, there are often to be detected variations of a more formal character. This is noticeably true of robins. It may almost be said that no two of them sing alike; while now and then their vagaries are conspicuous enough to attract general attention. One who was my neighbor last year interjected into his song a series of four or five most exact imitations of the peep of a chicken. When I first heard this performance, I was in company with two friends, both of whom noticed and laughed at it; and some days afterwards I visited the spot again, and found the bird still rehearsing the same ridiculous medley. I conjectured that he had been brought up near a hen-coop, and, moreover, had been so unfortunate as to lose his father before his notes had become thoroughly fixed; and then, being compelled to finish his musical education by himself, had taken a fancy to practice these chicken calls. This guess may not have been correct. All I can affirm is that he sang exactly as he might have been expected to do, on that supposition; but certainly the resemblance seemed too close to be accidental.

The variations of the wood thrush are fully as striking as those of the robin, and sometimes it is impossible not to feel that the artist is making a deliberate effort to do something out of the ordinary course, something better than he has ever done before. Now and then he prefaces his proper song with many disconnected, extremely staccato notes, following each other at very distant and unexpected intervals of pitch. It is this, I conclude, which is meant by some writer (who it is I cannot now remember) when he criticises the wood thrush for spending too much time in tuning his instrument. But the fault is the critic's, I think; to my ear these preliminaries sound rather like the recitative which goes before the grand aria.

Still another musician who delights to take liberties with his score is the towhee bunting, or chewink. Indeed, he carries the matter so far that sometimes it seems almost as if he suspected the proximity of some self-conceited ornithologist, and were determined, if possible, to make a fool of him. And for my part, being neither self conceited nor an ornithologist, I am willing to confess that I have once or twice been so badly deceived that now the mere sight of this Pipilo is, so to speak, a means of grace to me.

One more of these innovators (these heretics, as they are most likely called by their more conservative brethren) is the field sparrow, better known as Spizella pusilla. His usual song consists of a simple line of notes, beginning leisurely, but growing shorter and more rapid to the close. The voice is so smooth and sweet, and the acceleration so well managed, that, although the whole is commonly a strict monotone, the effect is not in the least monotonous. This song I once heard rendered in reverse order, with a result so strange that I did not suspect the identity of the author till I had crept up within sight of him. Another of these sparrows, who has passed the last two seasons in my neighborhood, habitually doubles the measure; going through it in the usual way, and then, just as you expect him to conclude, catching it up again, Da capo.

But birds like these are quite outdone by such species as the song sparrow, the white-eyed vireo, and the Western meadow-lark,—species of which we may say that each individual bird has a whole repertory of songs at his command. The song sparrow, who is the best known of the three, will repeat one melody perhaps a dozen times, then change it for a second, and in turn leave that for a third; as if he were singing hymns of twelve or fifteen stanzas each, and set each hymn to its appropriate tune. It is something well worth listening to, common though it is, and may easily suggest a number of questions about the origin and meaning of bird music.

The white-eyed vireo is a singer of astonishing spirit, and his sudden changes from one theme to another are sometimes almost startling. He is a skillful ventriloquist, also, and I remember one in particular who outwitted me completely. He was rehearsing a well-known strain, but at the end there came up from the bushes underneath a querulous call. At first I took it for granted that some other bird was in the underbrush; but the note was repeated too many times, and came in too exactly on the beat.

I have no personal acquaintance with the Western meadow-lark, but no less than twenty-six of his songs have been printed in musical notation, and these are said to be by no means all.[4]

Others of our birds have similar gifts, though no others, so far as I know, are quite so versatile as these three. Several of the warblers, for example, have attained to more than one set song, notwithstanding the deservedly small reputation of this misnamed family. I have myself heard the golden-crowned thrush, the black-throated green warbler, the black-throated blue, the yellow-rumped, and the chestnut-sided, sing two melodies each, while the blue golden-winged has at least three; and this, of course, without making anything of slight variations such

4. Mr. C. N. Allen, in Bulletin of the Nuttall Ornithological Club, July, 1881.

as all birds are more or less accustomed to indulge in. The best of the three songs of the blue golden-wing I have never heard except on one occasion, but then it was repeated for half an hour under my very eyes. It bore no resemblance to the common dsee, dsee, dsee, of the species, and would appear to be seldom used; for not only have I never heard it since, but none of the writers seem ever to have heard it at all. However, I still keep a careful description of it, which I took down on the spot, and which I expect some future golden-wing to verify.

But the most celebrated of the warblers in this regard is the golden-crowned thrush, otherwise called the oven-bird and the wood wagtail. His ordinary effort is one of the noisiest, least melodious, and most incessant sounds to be heard in our woods. His song is another matter. For that he takes to the air (usually starting from a tree-top, although I have seen him rise from the ground), whence, after a preliminary chip, chip, he lets fall a hurried flood of notes, in the midst of which can usually be distinguished his familiar weechee, weechee, weechee. It is nothing wonderful that he should sing on the wing,—many other birds do the same, and very much better than he; but he is singular in that he strictly reserves his aerial music for late in the afternoon. I have heard it as early as three o'clock, but never before that, and it is most common about sunset. Writers speak of it as limited to the season of courtship; but I have heard it almost daily till near the end of July, and once, for my special benefit, perhaps, it was given in full—and repeated—on the first day of September. But who taught the little creature to do this,—to sing one song in the forenoon, perched upon a twig, and to keep another for afternoon, singing that invariably on the wing? and what difference is there between the two in the mind of the singer?[5]

It is an indiscretion ever to say of a bird that he has only such and such notes. You may have been his friend for years, but the next time you go into the woods he will likely enough put you to shame by singing something not so much as hinted at in your description. I thought I knew the song of the yellow-rumped warbler, having listened to it many times,—a slight and rather characterless thing, nowise remarkable. But coming down Mount Willard one day in June, I heard a warbler's song

5. Since this paper was written I have three times heard the wood wagtail's true song in the morning,—but in neither case was the bird in the air. See p. 141.

which brought me to a sudden halt. It was new and beautiful,—more beautiful, it seemed at the moment, than any warbler's song I had ever heard. What could it be? A little patient waiting (while the black-flies and mosquitoes "came upon me to eat up my flesh"), and the wonderful stranger appeared in full view,—my old acquaintance, the yellow-rumped warbler.

With all this strong tendency on the part of birds to vary their music, how is it that there is still such a degree of uniformity, so that, as we have said, every species may be recognized by its notes? Why does every red-eyed vireo sing in one way, and every white-eyed vireo in another? Who teaches the young chipper to trill, and the young linnet to warble? In short, how do birds come by their music? Is it all a matter of instinct, inherited habit, or do they learn it? The answer appears to be that birds sing as children talk, by simple imitation. Nobody imagines that the infant is born with a language printed upon his brain. The father and mother may never have known a word of any tongue except the English, but if the child is brought up to hear only Chinese, he will infallibly speak that, and nothing else. And careful experiments have shown the same to be true of birds.[6] Taken from the nest just after they leave the shell, they invariably sing, not their own so-called natural song, but the song of their foster-parents; provided, of course, that this is not anything beyond their physical capacity. The notorious house sparrow (our "English" sparrow), in his wild or semi-domesticated state, never makes a musical sound; but if he is taken in hand early enough, he may be taught to sing, so it is said, nearly as well as the canary. Bechstein relates that a Paris clergyman had two of these sparrows whom he had trained to speak, and, among other things, to recite several of the shorter commandments; and the narrative goes on to say that it was sometimes very comical, when the pair were disputing over their food, to hear one gravely admonish the other, "Thou shalt not steal!" It would be interesting to know why creatures thus gifted do not sing of their own motion. With their amiability and sweet peaceableness they ought to be caroling the whole year round.

This question of the transmission of songs from one generation to

---

6. See the paper of Daines Barrington in Philosophical Transactions for 1773; also, Darwin's Descent of Man, and Wallace's Natural Selection.

another is, of course, a part of the general subject of animal intelligence, a subject much discussed in these days on account of its bearing upon the modern doctrine concerning the relation of man to the inferior orders.

We have nothing to do with such a theme, but it may not be out of place to suggest to preachers and moralists that here is a striking and unhackneyed illustration of the force of early training. Birds sing by imitation, it is true, but as a rule they imitate only the notes which they hear during the first few weeks after they are hatched. One of Mr. Barrington's linnets, for example, after being educated under a titlark, was put into a room with two birds of his own species, where he heard them sing freely every day for three months. He made no attempt to learn anything from them, however, but kept on practicing what the titlark had taught him, quite unconscious of anything singular or unpatriotic in such a course. This law, that impressions received during the immaturity of the powers become the unalterable habit of the after life, is perhaps the most momentous of all the laws in whose power we find ourselves. Sometimes we are tempted to call it cruel. But if it were annulled, this would be a strange world. What a hurly-hurly we should have among the birds! There would be no more telling them by their notes. Thrushes and jays, wrens and chickadees, finches and warblers, all would be singing one grand medley.

Between these two opposing tendencies, one urging to variation, the other to permanence (for Nature herself is half radical, half conservative), the language of birds has grown from rude beginnings to its present beautiful diversity; and whoever lives a century of millenniums hence will listen to music such as we in this day can only dream of. Inappreciably but ceaselessly the work goes on. Here and there is born a master-singer, a feathered genius, and every generation makes its own addition to the glorious inheritance.

It may be doubted whether there is any real connection between moral character and the possession of wings. Nevertheless there has long been a popular feeling that some such congruity does exist; and certainly it seems unreasonable to suppose that creatures who are able to soar at will into the heavens should be without other equally angelic attributes. But, be that as it may, our friends, the birds, do undeniably set us a good example in several respects. To mention only one, how becoming is their observance of morning and evening song! In spite of their industrious spirit (and few of us labor more hours daily), neither their first nor their last thoughts are given to the question, What shall we eat, and what shall we drink? Possibly their habit of saluting the rising and setting sun may be thought to favor the theory that the worship of the god of day was the original religion. I know nothing about that. But it would be a sad change if the birds, declining from their present beautiful custom, were to sleep and work, work and sleep, with no holy hour between, as is too much the case with the being who, according to his own pharisaic notion, is the only religious animal.

In the season, however, the woods are by no means silent, even at noonday. Many species (such as the vireos and warblers, who get their living amid the foliage of trees) sing as they work; while the thrushes and others, who keep business and pleasure more distinct, are often too happy to go many hours together without a hymn. I have even seen robins singing without quitting the turf; but that is rather unusual, for somehow birds have come to feel that they must get away from the ground when the lyrical mood is upon them. This may be a thing of sentiment (for is not language full of uncomplimentary allusions to earth and earthliness?); but more likely it is prudential. The gift of song is no doubt a dangerous blessing to creatures who have so many enemies, and we can readily believe that they have found it safer to be up where they can look about them while thus publishing their whereabouts.

A very interesting exception to this rule is the savanna sparrow, who sings habitually from the ground. But even he shares the common feeling, and stretches himself to his full height with an earnestness which is almost laughable, in view of the result; for his notes are hardly louder than a cricket's chirp. Probably he has fallen into this lowly habit from living in meadows and salt marshes, where bushes and trees are not readily to be come at; and it is worth noticing that, in the case of the skylark and the white-winged blackbird, the same conditions have led to a result precisely opposite. The sparrow, we may presume, was originally of a humble disposition, and when nothing better offered itself for a singing-perch easily grew accustomed to standing upon a stone or a little lump of earth; and this practice, long persisted in, naturally had the effect to lessen the loudness of his voice. The skylark, on the other hand, when he did not readily find a tree-top, said to himself, "Never mind! I have a pair of wings." And so the lark is famous, while the sparrow remains un heard-of, and is even mistaken for a grasshopper.

How true it is that the very things which dishearten one nature and break it down, only help another to find out what it was made for! If you would foretell the development, either of a bird or of a man, it is not enough to know his environment, you must know also what there is in him.

We have possibly made too much of the savanna sparrow's innocent eccentricity. He fills his place, and fills it well; and who knows but that he may yet outshine the skylark? There is a promise, I believe, for those who humble themselves. But what shall be said of species which do not even try to sing, and that, notwithstanding they have all the structural peculiarities of singing birds, and must, almost certainly, have come from ancestors who were singers? We have already mentioned the house sparrow, whose defect is the more mysterious on account of his belonging to so highly musical a family. But he was never accused of not being noisy enough, while we have one bird who, though he is classed with the oscines, passes his life in almost unbroken silence. Of course I refer to the waxwing, or cedar-bird, whose faint, sibilant whisper can scarcely be thought to contradict the foregoing description. By what strange freak he has lapsed into this ghostly habit, nobody knows. I make no account of the insinuation that he gave up music because it hindered his success in cherry-stealing. He likes cherries, it is true; and who can blame him? But he would need to work hard to steal more than does that indefatigable songster, the robin. I feel sure he has some better reason than this for his Quakerish conduct. But, however he came by his stillness, it is likely that by this time he plumes himself upon it. Silence is golden, he thinks, the supreme result of the highest æsthetic culture. Those loud creatures, the thrushes and finches! What a vulgar set they are, to be sure, the more's the pity! Certainly if he does not reason in some such way, bird nature is not so human as we have given it credit for being. Besides, the waxwing has an uncommon appreciation of the decorous; at least, we must think so if we are able to credit a story of Nuttall's. He declares that a Boston gentleman, whose name he gives, saw one of a company of these birds capture an insect, and offer it to his neighbor; he, however, delicately declined the dainty bit, and it was offered to the next, who, in turn, was equally polite; and the morsel actually passed back and forth along the line, till, finally, one of the flock was persuaded to eat it. I have never seen anything equal to this; but one day, happening to stop under a low cedar, I discovered right over my head a waxwing's nest with the mother-bird sitting upon it, while her mate was perched beside her on the branch. He was barely out of my reach, but he did not move a muscle; and although he uttered no sound, his behavior said as plainly as possible, "What do you expect to do here? Don't you see I am standing guard over this nest?" I should be ashamed not to be able to add that I respected his dignity and courage, and left him and his castle unmolested.

Observations so discursive as these can hardly be finished; they must break off abruptly, or else go on forever. Let us make an end, therefore, with expressing our hope that the cedar-bird, already so handsome and chivalrous, will yet take to himself a song; one sweet and original, worthy to go with his soft satin coat, his ornaments of sealing-wax, and his magnificent top-knot. Let him do that, and he shall always be made welcome; yes, even though he come in force and in cherry-time.

CHARACTER IN FEATHERS.

The finger of God hath left an inscription upon all his works, not graphical or composed of letters, but of their several forms, constitutions, parts, and operations, which, aptly joined together, do make one word that doth express their natures. By these letters God calls the stars by their names; and by this alphabet Adam assigned to every creature a name peculiar to its nature.

— Sir Thomas Browne.

CHARACTER IN FEATHERS.

In this economically governed world the same thing serves many uses. Who will take upon himself to enumerate the offices of sunlight, or water, or indeed of any object whatever? Because we know it to be good for this or that, it by no means follows that we have discovered what it was made for. What we have found out is perhaps only something by the way; as if a man should think the sun were created for his own private convenience. In some moods it seems doubtful whether we are yet acquainted with the real value of anything. But, be that as it may, we need not scruple to admire so much as our ignorance permits us to see of the workings of this divine frugality. The piece of woodland, for instance, which skirts the village,—how various are its ministries to the inhabitants, each of whom, without forethought or question, takes the benefit proper to himself! The poet saunters there as in a true Holy Land, to have his heart cooled and stilled. Mr. A. and Mr. B., who hold the deeds of the "property," walk through it to look at the timber, with an eye to dollars and cents. The botanist has his errand there, the zoölogist his, and the child his. Oftenest of all, perhaps (for barbarism dies hard, and even yet the ministers of Christ find it a capital sport to murder small fishes),—oftenest of all comes the man, poor soul, who thinks of the forest as of a place to which he may go when he wishes to amuse himself by killing something. Meanwhile, the rabbits and the squirrels, the hawks and the owls, look upon all such persons as no better than intruders (do not the woods belong to those who live in them?); while nobody remembers the meteorologist, who nevertheless smiles in his sleeve at all these one-sided notions, and says to himself that he knows the truth of the matter.

So is it with everything; and with all the rest, so is it with the birds. The interest they excite is of all grades, from that which looks upon them as items of millinery, up to that of the makers of ornithological systems, who ransack the world for specimens, and who have no doubt that the chief end of a bird is to be named and catalogued,—the more synonyms the better. Somewhere between these two extremes comes the person whose interest in birds is friendly rather than scientific; who has little taste for shooting, and an aversion from dissecting; who delights in the living creatures themselves, and counts a bird in the bush worth two in the hand. Such a person, if he is intelligent, makes good use of the best works on ornithology; he would not know how to get along without them; but he studies most the birds themselves, and after a while he begins to associate them on a plan of his own. Not that he distrusts the approximate correctness of the received classification, or ceases to find it of daily service; but though it were as accurate as the multiplication table, it is based (and rightly, no doubt) on anatomical structure alone; it rates birds as bodies, and nothing else: while to the person of whom we are speaking birds are, first of all, souls; his interest in them is, as we say, personal; and we are none of us in the habit of grouping our friends according to height, or complexion, or any other physical peculiarity.

But it is not proposed in this paper to attempt a new classification of any sort, even the most unscientific and fanciful. All I am to do is to set down at random a few studies in such a method as I have indicated; in short, a few studies in the temperaments of birds. Nor, in making this attempt, am I unmindful how elusive of analysis traits of character are, and how diverse is the impression which the same personality produces upon different observers. In matters of this kind every judgment is largely a question of emphasis and proportion; and, moreover, what we find in our friends depends in great part on what we have in ourselves. This I do not forget; and therefore I foresee that others will discover in the birds of whom I write many things that I miss, and perhaps will miss some things which I have treated as patent or even conspicuous.

It remains only for each to testify what he has seen, and at the end to confess that a soul, even the soul of a bird, is after all a mystery.

Let our first example, then, be the common black-capped titmouse, or chickadee. He is, par excellence, the bird of the merry heart. There is a notion current, to be sure, that all birds are merry; but that is one of those second-hand opinions which a man who begins to observe for himself soon finds it necessary to give up. With many birds life is a hard struggle. Enemies are numerous, and the food supply is too often scanty. Of some species it is probable that very few die in their beds. But the chickadee seems to be exempt from all forebodings. His coat is thick, his heart is brave, and, whatever may happen, something will be found to eat. "Take no thought for the morrow" is his creed, which he accepts, not "for substance of doctrine," but literally. No matter how bitter the wind or how deep the snow, you will never find the chickadee, as the saying is, under the weather. It is this perennial good humor, I suppose, which makes other birds so fond of his companionship; and their example might well be heeded by persons who suffer from fits of depression. Such unfortunates could hardly do better than to court the society of the joyous tit. His whistles and chirps, his graceful feats of climbing and hanging, and withal his engaging familiarity (for, of course, such good-nature as his could not consist with suspiciousness) would most likely send them home in a more Christian mood. The time will come, we may hope, when doctors will prescribe bird-gazing instead of blue-pill.

To illustrate the chickadee's trustfulness, I may mention that a friend of mine captured one in a butterfly-net, and, carrying him into the house, let him loose in the sitting-room. The little stranger was at home immediately, and seeing the window full of plants, proceeded to go over them carefully, picking off the lice with which such window-gardens are always more or less infested. A little later he was taken into my friend's lap, and soon he climbed up to his shoulder; where, after hopping about for a few minutes on his coat-collar, he selected a com fortable roosting place, tucked his head under his wing, and went to sleep, and slept on undisturbed while carried from one room to another. Probably the chickadee's nature is not of the deepest. I have never seen him when his joy rose to ecstasy. Still his feelings are not shallow, and the faithfulness of the pair to each other and to their offspring is of the highest order. The female has sometimes to be taken off the nest, and even to be held in the hand, before the eggs can be examined.

Our American goldfinch is one of the loveliest of birds. With his elegant plumage, his rhythmical, undulatory flight, his beautiful song, and his more beautiful soul, he ought to be one of the best beloved, if not one of the most famous; but he has never yet had half his deserts. He is like the chickadee, and yet different. He is not so extremely confiding, nor should I call him merry. But he is always cheerful, in spite of his so-called plaintive note, from which he gets one of his names, and always amiable. So far as I know, he never utters a harsh sound; even the young ones, asking for food, use only smooth, musical tones. During the pairing season his delight often becomes rapturous. To see him then, hovering and singing,—or, better still, to see the devoted pair hovering together, billing and singing,—is enough to do even a cynic good. The happy lovers! They have never read it in a book, but it is written on their hearts,—

"The gentle law, that each should be
The other's heaven and harmony."

The goldfinch has the advantage of the titmouse in several respects, but he lacks that sprightliness, that exceeding light-heartedness, which is the chickadee's most endearing characteristic.

For the sake of a strong contrast, we may look next at the brown thrush, known to farmers as the planting-bird and to ornithologists as Harporhynchus rufus; a staid and solemn Puritan, whose creed is the Preacher's,—"Vanity of vanities, all is vanity." No frivolity and merry-making for him! After his brief annual period of intensely passionate song, he does penance for the remainder of the year,—skulking about, on the ground or near it, silent and gloomy. He seems ever on the watch against an enemy, and, unfortunately for his comfort, he has nothing of the reckless, bandit spirit, such as the jay possesses, which goes to make a moderate degree of danger almost a pastime. Not that he is without courage; when his nest is in question he will take great risks; but in general his manner is dispirited, "sicklied o'er with the pale cast of thought." Evidently he feels

"The heavy and the weary weight
Of all this unintelligible world;"

and it would not be surprising if he sometimes raised the question, "Is life worth living?" It is the worst feature of his case that his melancholy is not of the sort which softens and refines the nature. There is no suggestion of saintliness about it. In fact, I am convinced that this long-tailed thrush has a constitutional taint of vulgarity. His stealthy, underhand manner is one mark of this, and the same thing comes out again in his music. Full of passion as his singing is (and we have hardly anything to compare with it in this regard), yet the listener cannot help smiling now and then; the very finest passage is followed so suddenly by some uncouth guttural note, or by some whimsical drop from the top to the bottom of the scale.

In neighborly association with the brown thrush is the towhee bunting, or chewink. The two choose the same places for their summer homes, and, unless I am deceived, they often migrate in company. But though they are so much together, and in certain of their ways very much alike, their habits of mind are widely dissimilar. The towhee is of a peculiarly even disposition. I have seldom heard him scold, or use any note less good-natured and musical than his pleasant cherawink. I have never detected him in a quarrel such as nearly all birds are once in a while guilty of, ungracious as it may seem to mention the fact; nor have I ever seen him hopping nervously about and twitching his tail, as is the manner of most species, when, for instance, their nests are approached. Nothing seems to annoy him. At the same time, he is not full of continual merriment like the chickadee, nor occasionally in a rapture like the goldfinch. Life with him is pitched in a low key; comfortable rather than cheerful, and never jubilant. And yet, for all the towhee's careless demeanor, you soon begin to suspect him of being deep. He appears not to mind you; he keeps on scratching among the dry leaves as if he had no thought of being driven away by your presence; but in a minute or two you look that way again, and he is not there. If you pass near his nest, he makes not a tenth part of the ado which a brown thrush would make in the same circumstances, but (partly for this reason) you will find half a dozen nests of the thrush sooner than one of his. With all his simplicity and frankness, which puts him in happy contrast with the thrush, he knows as well as anybody how to keep his own counsel. I have seen him with his mate for two or three days together about the flower-beds in the Boston Public Garden, and so far as appeared they were feeding as unconcernedly as though they had been on their own native heath, amid the scrub-oaks and huckleberry bushes; but after their departure it was remembered that they had not once been heard to utter a sound. If self-possession be four fifths of good manners, our red-eyed Pipilo may certainly pass for a gentleman.

We have now named four birds, the chickadee, the goldfinch, the brown thrush, and the towhee,—birds so diverse in plumage that no eye could fail to discriminate them at a glance. But the four differ no more truly in bodily shape and dress than they do in that inscrutable something which we call temperament, disposition. If the soul of each were separated from the body and made to stand out in sight, those of us who have really known the birds in the flesh would have no difficulty in saying, This is the titmouse, and this the towhee. It would be with them as we hope it will be with our friends in the next world, whom we shall recognize there because we knew them here; that is, we knew them, and not merely the bodies they lived in. This kind of familiarity with birds has no necessary connection with ornithology. Personal intimacy and a knowledge of anatomy are still two different things. As we have all heard, ours is an age of science; but, thank fortune, matters have not yet gone so far that a man must take a course in anthropology before he can love his neighbor.

It is a truth only too patent that taste and conscience are sometimes at odds. One man wears his faults so gracefully that we can hardly help falling in love with them, while another, alas, makes even virtue itself repulsive. I am moved to this commonplace reflection by thinking of the blue jay, a bird of doubtful character, but one for whom, nevertheless, it is impossible not to feel a sort of affection and even of respect. He is quite as suspicious as the brown thrush, and his instinct for an invisible perch is perhaps as unerring as the cuckoo's; and yet, even when he takes to hiding, his manner is not without a dash of boldness. He has a most irascible temper, also, but, unlike the thrasher, he does not allow his ill-humor to degenerate into chronic sulkiness. Instead, he flies into a furious passion, and is done with it. Some say that on such occasions he swears, and I have myself seen him when it was plain that nothing except a natural impossibility kept him from tearing his hair. His larynx would make him a singer, and his mental capacity is far above the average; but he has perverted his gifts, till his music is nothing but noise and his talent nothing but smartness. A like process of depravation the world has before now witnessed in political life, when a man of brilliant natural endowments has yielded to low ambitions and stooped to unworthy means, till what was meant to be a statesman turns put to be a demagogue. But perhaps we wrong our handsome friend, fallen angel though he be, to speak thus of him. Most likely he would resent the comparison, and I do not press it. We must admit that juvenile sportsmen have persecuted him unduly; and when a creature cannot show himself without being shot at, he may be pardoned for a little misanthropy. Christians as we are, how many of us could stand such a test? In these circumstances, it is a point in the jay's favor that he still has, what is rare with birds, a sense of humor, albeit it is humor of a rather grim sort,—the sort which expends itself in practical jokes and uncivil epithets. He has discovered the school-boy's secret: that for the expression of unadulterated derision there is nothing like the short sound of a, prolonged into a drawl. Yah, yah, he cries; and sometimes, as you enter the woods, you may hear him shouting so as to be heard for half a mile, "Here comes a fool with a gun; look out for him!"

It is natural to think of the shrike in connection with the jay, but the two have points of unlikeness no less than of resemblance. The shrike is a taciturn bird. If he were a politician, he would rely chiefly on what is known as the "still hunt," although he too can scream loudly enough on occasion. His most salient trait is his impudence, but even that is of a negative type. "Who are you," he says, "that I should be at the trouble to insult you?" He has made a study of the value of silence as an indication of contempt, and is almost human in his ability to stare straight by a person whose presence it suits him to ignore. His imperturbability is wonderful. Watch him as closely as you please, you will never discover what he is thinking about. Undertake, for instance, now that the fellow is singing from the top of a small tree only a few rods from where you are standing,—undertake to settle the long dispute whether his notes are designed to decoy small birds within his reach. Those whistles and twitters,—hear them! So miscellaneous! so different from anything which would be expected from a bird of his size and general disposition! so very like the notes of sparrows! They must be imitative. You begin to feel quite sure of it. But just at this point the sounds cease, and you look up to discover that Collurio has fallen to preening his feathers in the most listless manner imaginable. "Look at me," he says; "do I act like one on the watch for his prey? Indeed, sir, I wish the innocent sparrows no harm; and besides, if you must know it, I ate an excellent game-breakfast two hours ago, while laggards like you were still abed." In the winter, which is the only season when I have been able to observe him, the shrike is to the last degree unsocial, and I have known him to stay for a month in one spot all by himself, spending a good part of every day perched upon a telegraph wire. He ought not to be very happy, with such a disposition, one would think; but he seems to be well contented, and sometimes his spirits are fairly exuberant. Perhaps, as the phrase is, he enjoys himself; in which case he certainly has the advantage of most of us,—unless, indeed, we are easily pleased. At any rate, he is philosopher enough to appreciate the value of having few wants; and I am not sure but that he anticipated the vaunted discovery of Teufelsdröckh, that the fraction of life may be increased by lessening the denominator. But even the stoical shrike is not without his epicurean weakness. When he has killed a sparrow, he eats the brains first; after that, if he is still hungry, he devours the coarser and less savory parts. In this, however, he only shares the well-nigh universal inconsistency. There are never many thorough-going stoics in the world. Epictetus declared with an oath that he should be glad to see one.[7] To take everything as equally good, to know no difference between bitter and sweet, penury and plenty, slander and praise,—this is a great attainment, a Nirvana to which few can hope to arrive. Some wise man has said (and the remark has more meaning than may at once appear) that dying is usually one of the last things which men do in this world.

Against the foil of the butcher-bird's stolidity we may set the inquisitive, garrulous temperament of the white-eyed vireo and the yellow-breasted chat. The vireo is hardly larger than the goldfinch, but let him be in one of his conversational moods, and he will fill a smilax thicket with noise enough for two or three cat-birds. Meanwhile he keeps his eye upon you, and seems to be inviting your attention to his

7. This does not harmonize exactly with a statement which Emerson makes somewhere, to the effect that all the stoics were stoics indeed. But Epictetus had never lived in Concord.

loquacious abilities. The chat is perhaps even more voluble. Staccato whistles and snarls follow each other at most extraordinary intervals of pitch, and the attempt at showing off is sometimes unmistakable. Occasionally he takes to the air, and flies from one tree to another; teetering his body and jerking his tail, in an indescribable fashion, and chattering all the while. His "inner consciousness" at such a moment would be worth perusing. Possibly he has some feeling for the grotesque. But I suspect not; probably what we laugh at as the antics of a clown is all sober earnest to him.

At best, it is very little we can know about what is passing in a bird's mind. We label him with two or three sesquipedalia verba, give his territorial range, describe his notes and his habits of nidification, and fancy we have rendered an account of the bird. But how should we like to be inventoried in such a style? "His name was John Smith; he lived in Boston, in a three-story brick house; he had a baritone voice, but was not a good singer." All true enough; but do you call that a man's biography?

The four birds last spoken of are all wanting in refinement. The jay and the shrike are wild and rough, not to say barbarous, while the white-eyed vireo and the chat have the character which commonly goes by the name of oddity. All four are interesting for their strong individuality and their picturesqueness, but it is a pleasure to turn from them to creatures like our four common New England Hylocichlæ, or small thrushes. These are the real patricians. With their modest but rich dress, and their dignified, quiet demeanor, they stand for the true aristocratic spirit. Like all genuine aristocrats, they carry an air of distinction, of which no one who approaches them can long remain unconscious. When you go into their haunts they do not appear so much frightened as offended. "Why do you intrude?" they seem to say; "these are our woods;" and they bow you out with all ceremony. Their songs are in keeping with this character; leisurely, unambitious, and brief, but in beauty of voice and in high musical quality excelling all other music of the woods. However, I would not exaggerate, and I have not found even these thrushes perfect. The hermit, who is my favorite of the four, has a habit of slowly raising and depressing his tail when his mind is disturbed—a trick of which it is likely he is unconscious, but which, to say the least, is not a mark of good breeding; and the Wilson, while every note of his song breathes of spirituality, has nevertheless a most vulgar alarm call, a petulant, nasal, one-syllabled yeork. I do not know anything so grave against the wood thrush or the Swainson; although when I have fooled the former with decoy whistles, I have found him more inquisitive than seemed altogether becoming to a bird of his quality. But character without flaw is hardly to be insisted on by sons of Adam, and, after all deductions are made, the claim of the Hylocichlæ to noble blood can never be seriously disputed. I have spoken of the four together, but each is clearly distinguished from all the others; and this I believe to be as true of mental traits as it is of details of plumage and song. No doubt, in general, they are much alike; we may say that they have the same qualities; but a close acquaintance will reveal that the qualities have been mixed in different proportions, so that the total result in each case is a personality strictly unique.

And what is true of the Hylocichlæ is true of every bird that flies. Anatomy and dress and even voice aside, who does not feel the dissimilarity between the cat-bird and the robin, and still more the difference, amounting to contrast, between the cat-bird and the bluebird? Distinctions of color and form are what first strike the eye, but on better acquaintance these are felt to be superficial and comparatively unimportant; the difference is not one of outside appearance. It is his gentle, high-bred manner and not his azure coat, which makes the bluebird; and the cat-bird would be a cat-bird in no matter what garb, so long as he retained his obtrusive self-consciousness and his prying, busy-body spirit; all of which, being inter preted, comes, it may be, to no more than this, "Fine feathers don't make fine birds."

Even in families containing many closely allied species, I believe that every species has its own proper character, which sufficient intercourse would enable us to make a due report of. Nobody ever saw a song-sparrow manifesting the spirit of a chipper, and I trust it will not be in my day that any of our American sparrows are found emulating the virtues of their obstreperous immigrant cousin. Of course it is true of birds, as of men, that some have much more individuality than others. But know any bird or any man well enough, and he will prove to be himself, and nobody else. To know the ten thousand birds of the world well enough to see how, in bodily structure, habit of life, and mental characteristics, every one is different from every other is the long and delightful task which is set before the ornithologist.

But this is not all. The ornithology of the future must be ready to give an answer to the further question how these divergences of anatomy and temperament originated. How came the chickadee by his endless fund of happy spirits? Whence did the towhee derive his equanimity, and the brown thrush his saturnine temper? The waxwing and the vireo have the same vocal organs; why should the first do nothing but whisper, while the second is so loud and voluble? Why is one bird belligerent and another peaceable; one barbarous and another civilized; one grave and another gay? Who can tell? We can make here and there a plausible conjecture. We know that the behavior of the blue jay varies greatly in different parts of the country, in consequence of the different treatment which he receives. We judge that the chickadee, from the peculiarity of his feeding habits, is more certain than most birds are of finding a meal whenever he is hungry; and that, we are assured from experience, goes a long way toward making a body contented. We think it likely that the brown thrush is at some special disadvantage in this respect, or has some peculiar enemies warring upon him; in which case it is no more than we might expect that he should be a pessimist. And, with all our ignorance, we are yet sure that everything has a cause, and we would fain hold by the brave word of Emerson, "Undoubtedly we have no questions to ask which are unanswerable."

IN THE WHITE MOUNTAINS

Our music's in the hills.

— Emerson.

IN THE WHITE MOUNTAINS.

It was early in June when I set out for my third visit to the White Mountains, and the ticket-seller and the baggage-master in turn assured me that the Crawford House, which I named as my destination, was not yet open. They spoke, too, in the tone which men use when they mention something which, but for uncommon stupidity, you would have known beforehand. The kindly sarcasm missed its mark, however. I was aware that the hotel was not yet ready for the "general public." But I said to myself that, for once at least, I was not to be included in that unfashionably promiscuous company. The vulgar crowd must wait, of course. For the present the mountains, in reporters' language, were "on private view;" and despite the ignorance of railway officials, I was one of the elect. In plainer phrase, I had in my pocket a letter from the manager of the famous inn before mentioned, in which he promised to do what he could for my entertainment, even though he was not yet, as he said, keeping a hotel.

Possibly I made too much of a small matter; but it pleased me to feel that this visit of mine was to be of a peculiarly intimate character,—almost, indeed, as if Mount Washington himself had bidden me to private audience.

Compelled to wait three or four hours in North Conway, I improved the opportunity to stroll once more down into the lovely Saco meadows, whose "green felicity" was just now at its height. Here, perched upon a fence-rail, in the shadow of an elm, I gazed at the snow-crowned Mount Washington range, while the bobolinks and savanna sparrows made music on every side. The song of the bobolinks dropped from above, and the microphonic tune of the sparrows came up from the grass,—sky and earth keeping holiday together. Almost I could have believed myself in Eden. But, alas, even the birds themselves were long since shut out of that garden of innocence, and as I started back toward the village a crow went hurrying past me, with a kingbird in hot pursuit. The latter was more fortunate than usual, or more plucky; actually alighting on the crow's back and riding for some distance. I could not distinguish his motions,—he was too far away for that,—but I wished him joy of his victory, and grace to improve it to the full. For it is scandalous that a bird of the crow's cloth should be a thief; and so, although I reckon him among my friends,—in truth, because I do so,—I am always able to take it patiently when I see him chastised for his fault. Imperfect as we all know each other to be, it is a comfort to feel that few of us are so altogether bad as not to take more or less pleasure in seeing a neighbor's character improved under a course of moderately painful discipline.

At Bartlett word came that the passenger car would go no further, but that a freight train would soon start, on which, if I chose, I could continue my journey. Accordingly, I rode up through the Notch on a platform car,—a mode of conveyance which I can heartily and in all good conscience recommend. There is no crowd of exclaiming tourists, the train of necessity moves slowly, and the open platform offers no obstruction to the view. For a time I had a seat, which after a little two strangers ventured to occupy with me; for "it's an ill wind that blows nobody good," and there happened to be on the car one piece of baggage,—a coffin, inclosed in a pine box. Our sitting upon it could not harm either it or us; nor did we wean any disrespect to the man, whoever he might be, whose body was to be buried in it. Judging the dead charitably, as in duty bound, I had no doubt he would have been glad if he could have seen his "narrow house" put to such a use. So we made ourselves comfortable with it, until, at an invisible station, it was taken off. Then we were obliged to stand, or to retreat into a miserable small box-car behind us. The platform would lurch a little now and then, and I, for one, was not experienced as a "train hand;" but we all kept our places till the Frankenstein trestle was reached. Here, where for five hundred feet we could look down upon the jagged rocks eighty feet below us, one of the trio suddenly had an errand into the box-car aforesaid, leaving the platform to the other stranger and me. All in all, the ride through the Notch had never before been so enjoyable,

I thought; and late in the evening I found myself once again at the Crawford House, and in one of the best rooms,—as well enough I might be, being the only guest in the house.

The next morning, before it was really light, I was lying awake looking at Mount Webster, while through the open window came the loud, cheery song of the white-throated sparrows. The hospitable creatures seemed to be inviting me to come at once into their woods; but I knew only too well that, if the invitation were accepted, they would every one of them take to hiding like bashful children.

The white-throat is one of the birds for whom I cherish a special liking. On my first trip to the mountains I jumped off the train for a moment at Bartlett, and had hardly touched the ground before I heard his familiar call. Here, then, was Mr. Peabody at home. Season after season he had camped near me in Massachusetts, and many a time I had been gladdened by his lively serenade; now he greeted me from his own native woods. So far as my observations have gone, he is common throughout the mountain region; and that in spite of the standard guide-book, which puts him down as patronizing the Glen House almost exclusively. He knows the routes too well to need any guide, however, and may be excused for his ignorance of the official programme. It is wonderful how shy he is,—the more wonderful, because, during his migrations, his manner is so very different. Then, even in a city park you may watch him at your leisure, while his loud, clear whistle is often to be heard rising above a din of horse-cars and heavy wagons. But here, in his summer quarters, you will listen to his song a hundred times before you once catch a glimpse of the singer. At first thought it seems strange that a bird should be most at home when he is away from home; but in the one case he has nothing but his own safety to consult, while in the other he is thinking of those whose lives are more to him than his own, and whose hiding-place he is every moment on the alert to conceal.

In Massachusetts we do not expect to find sparrows in deep woods. They belong in fields and pastures, in roadside thickets, or by fence-rows and old stone-walls bordered with barberry bushes and alders. But these white-throats are children of the wilderness. It is one charm of their music that it always comes, or seems to come, from such a distance,—from far up the mountain-side, or from the inaccessible depths of some ravine. I shall not soon forget its wild beauty as it rose out of the spruce forests below me, while I was enjoying an evening promenade, all by myself, over the long, flat summit of Moosilauke. From his habit of singing late at night this sparrow is in some places known as the nightingale. His more common name is the Peabody bird; while a Jefferson man, who was driving me over the Cherry Mountain road, called him the Peverly bird, and told me the following story:—

A farmer named Peverly was walking about his fields one spring morning, trying to make up his mind whether the time had come to put in his wheat. The question was important, and he was still in a deep quandary, when a bird spoke up out of the wood and said, "Sow wheat, Peverly, Peverly, Peverly!—Sow wheat, Peverly, Peverly, Peverly!" That settled the matter. The wheat was sown, and in the fall a most abundant harvest was gathered; and ever since then this little feathered oracle has been known as the Peverly bird.

We have improved on the custom of the ancients: they examined a bird's entrails; we listen to his song. Who says the Yankee is not wiser than the Greek?

But I was lying abed in the Crawford House when the voice of Zonotrichia albicollis sent my thoughts thus astray, from Moosilauke to Delphi. That day and the two following were passed in roaming about the woods near the hotel. The pretty painted trillium was in blossom, as was also the dark purple species, and the hobble-bush showed its broad white cymes in all directions. Here and there was the modest little spring beauty (Claytonia Caroliniana), and not far from the Elephant's Head I discovered my first and only patch of dicentra, with its delicate dissected leaves and its oddly shaped petals of white and pale yellow. The false mitrewort (Tiarella cordifolia) was in flower likewise, and the spur which is cut off Mount Willard by the railroad was all aglow with rhodora,—a perfect flower-garden, on the monochromatic plan now so much in vogue. Along the edge of the rocks on the summit of Mount Willard a great profusion of the common saxifrage was waving in the fresh breeze:

"Ten thousand saw I at a glance,

Tossing their heads in sprightly dance."

On the lower parts of the mountains, the foliage was already well out, while the upper parts were of a fine purplish tint, which at first I was unable to account for, but which I soon discovered to be due to the fact that the trees at that height were still only in bud.

A notable feature of the White Mountain forests is the absence of oaks and hickories. These tough, hard woods would seem to have been created on purpose to stand against wind and cold. But no; the hills are covered with the fragile poplars and birches and spruces, with never an oak or hickory among them. I suspect, indeed, that it is the very softness of the former which gives them their advantage. For this, as I suppose, is correlated with rapid growth; and where the summer is very short, speed may count for more than firmness of texture, especially during the first one or two years of the plant's life. Trees, like men, lose in one way what they gain in another; or, in other words, they "have the defects of their qualities." Probably Paul's confession, "When I am weak, then am I strong," is after all only the personal statement of a general law, as true of a poplar as of a Christian. For we all believe (do we not?) that the world is a universe, governed throughout by one Mind, so that whatever holds in one part is good everywhere.

But it was June, and the birds, who were singing from daylight till dark, would have the most of my attention. It was pleasant to find here two comparatively rare warblers, of whom I had before had only casual glimpses,—the mourning warbler and the bay-breasted. The former was singing his loud but commonplace ditty within a few rods of the piazza on one side of the house, while his congener, the Maryland yellow-throat, was to be heard on the other side, along with the black-cap (Dendrœca striata), the black-and-yellow, and the Canadian flycatcher. The mourning warbler's song, as I heard it, was like this: Whit whit whit, wit wit. The first three notes were deliberate and loud, on one key, and without accent. The last two were pitched a little lower, and were shorter, with the accent on the first of the pair; they were thinner in tone than the opening triplet, as is meant to be indicated by the dif ference of spelling.[8] Others of the family were the golden-crowned thrush, the small-billed water-thrush, the yellow-rumped, the Blackburnian (with his characteristic zillup, zillup, zillup), the black-throated green, the black-throated blue (the last with his loud, coarse kree, kree, kree),

---

8. He is said to have another song, beautiful and wren-like; but that I have never heard.

the redstart, and the elegant blue yellow-back. Altogether, they were a gorgeous company.

But the chief singers were the olive-backed thrushes and the winter wrens. I should be glad to know on just what principle the olive-backs and their near relatives, the hermits, distribute themselves throughout the mountain region. Each species seems to have its own sections, to which it returns year after year, and the olive-backed, being, as is well known, the more northern species of the two, naturally prefers the more elevated situations. I have found the latter abundant near the Profile House, and for three seasons it has had exclusive possession of the White Mountain Notch,—so far, at least, as I have been able to discover.[9] The hermits, on the other hand, frequent such places as North Conway, Gorham, Jefferson, Bethlehem, and the vicinity of the Flume. Only once have I found the two species in the same neighborhood. That was near the Breezy Point House, on the side of Mount Moosilauke; but this place is so peculiarly romantic, with its noble amphitheatre of hills, that I could not wonder neither species was willing to yield the ground entirely to the other; and even here it was to be noticed that the hermits were in or near the sugar-grove, while the Swainsons were in the forest, far off in an opposite direction.[10]

It is these birds, if any, whose music reaches the ears of the ordinary mountain tourist. Every man who is known among his acquaintances to have a little knowledge of such things is approached now and then with the question, "What bird was it, Mr. So-and-So, that I heard singing up in the mountains? I didn't see him; he was always ever so far off; but his voice was wonderful, so sweet and clear and loud!" As a rule it may safely be taken for granted that such interrogatories refer either to the Swainson thrush or to the hermit. The inquirer is very likely disposed to be incredulous when he is told that there are birds in his own woods whose voice is so like that of his admired New Hampshire songster that, if he were to hear the two together, he would not at first be able to tell

9. This is making no account of the gray-cheeked thrushes, who are found only near the tops of the mountains.

10. I have since found both species at Willoughby Lake, Vermont and the veery with them.

the one from the other. He has never heard them, he protests; which is true enough, for he never goes into the woods of his own town, or, if by chance he does, he leaves his ears behind him in the shop. His case is not peculiar. Men and women gaze enraptured at New Hampshire sunsets. How glorious they are, to be sure! What a pity the sun does not sometimes set in Massachusetts!

As a musician the olive-back is certainly inferior to the hermit, and, according to my taste, he is surpassed also by the wood thrush and the Wilson; but he is a magnificent singer, for all that, and when he is heard in the absence of the others it is often hard to believe that any one of them could do better. A good idea of the rhythm and length of his song may be gained by pronouncing somewhat rapidly the words, "I love, I love, I love you," or, as it sometimes runs, "I love, I love, I love you truly." How literal this translation is I am not scholar enough to determine, but without question it gives the sense substantially.

The winter wrens were less numerous than the thrushes, I think, but, like them, they sang at all hours of the day, and seemed to be well distributed throughout the woods. We can hardly help asking how it is that two birds so very closely related as the house wren and the winter wren should have been chosen haunts so extremely diverse,—the one preferring door-yards in thickly settled villages, the other keeping strictly to the wildest of all wild places. But whatever the explanation, we need not wish the fact itself different. Comparatively few ever hear the winter wren's song, to be sure (for you will hardly get it from a hotel piazza), but it is not the less enjoyed on that account. There is such a thing as a bird's making himself too common; and probably it is true even of the great prima donna that it is not those who live in the house with her who find most pleasure in her music. Moreover, there is much in time and circumstance. You hear a song in the village street, and pass along unmoved; but stand in the silence of the forest, with your feet in a bed of creeping snowberry and oxalis, and the same song goes to your very soul.

The great distinction of the winter wren's melody is its marked rhythm and accent, which give it a martial, fife-like character. Note tumbles over note in the true wren manner, and the strain comes to an end so suddenly that for the first few times you are likely to think that the bird has been interrupted. In the middle is a long in-drawn note, much like one of the canary's. The odd little creature does not get far away from the ground. I have never seen him sing from a living tree or bush, but always from a stump or a log, or from the root or branch of an overturned tree,—from something, at least, of nearly his own color [11] The song is intrinsically one of the most beautiful, and in my ears it has the further merit of being forever associated with reminiscences of ramblings among the White Hills. How well I remember an early morning hour at Profile Lake, when it came again and again across the water from the woods on Mount Cannon, under the Great Stone Face!

Whichever way I walked, I was sure of the society of the snow-birds. They hopped familiarly across the railroad track in front of the Crawford House, and on the summit of Mount Washington were scurrying about among the rocks, opening and shutting their pretty white-bordered fans. Half-way up Mount Willard I sat down to rest on a stone, and after a minute or two out dropped a snow-bird at my feet, and ran across the road, trailing her wings. I looked under the bank for her nest, but, to my surprise, could find nothing of it. So I made sure of knowing the place again, and continued my tramp. Returning two hours later, I sat down upon the same bowlder, and watched for the bird to appear as before; but she had gathered courage from my former failure,—or so it seemed,—and I waited in vain till I rapped upon the ground over her head. Then she scrambled out and limped away, repeating her innocent but hackneyed ruse. This time I was resolved not to be baffled. The nest was there, and I would find it. So down on my knees I got, and scrutinized the whole place most carefully. But though I had marked the precise spot, there was no sign of a nest. I was about giving over the search ignominiously, when I descried a slight opening between the overhanging roof of the bank and a layer of earth which some roots held in place close under it. Into this slit I inserted my fingers, and there, entirely out of sight, was the nest full of eggs. No man could ever have found it, had the bird been brave and wise enough to keep her seat. However, I had before this noticed that the snow-bird, while often extremely clever in choosing a building site, is seldom very

---

11. True when written, but now needing to be qualified by one exception. See p. 113.

skillful in keeping a secret. I saw him one day standing on the side of the same Mount Willard road,[12] gesticu lating and scolding with all his might, as much, as to say, "Please don't stop here! Go straight along, I beg of you! Our nest is right under this bank!" And one glance under the bank showed that I had not misinterpreted his demonstrations. For all that, I do not feel like taking a lofty tone in passing judgment upon Junco. He is not the only one whose wisdom is mixed with foolishness. There is at least one other person of whom the same is true,—a person of whom I have nevertheless a very good opinion, and with whom I am, or ought to be, better acquainted than I am with any animal that wears feathers.

The prettiest snow-bird's nest I ever saw was built beside the Crawford bridle path, on Mount Clinton, just before the path comes out of the woods at the top. It was lined with hair-moss (a species of Polytrichum) of a bright orange color, and with its four or five white, lilac-spotted eggs made so attractive a picture that I was constrained to pause a moment to look at it, even though I had three miles of a steep, rough footpath to descend, with a shower threatening to overtake me before I could reach the bottom. I wondered whether the architects really possessed an eye for color, or had only stumbled upon this elegant bit of decoration. On the whole, it seemed more charitable to conclude the former; and not only more charitable, but more scientific as well. For, if I understand the matter aright, Mr. Darwin and his followers have settled upon the opinion that birds do display an unmistakable fondness for bright tints; that, indeed, the males of many species wear brilliant plumage for no other reason than that their mates prefer them in that dress. Moreover, if a bird in New South Wales adorns

---

12. Beside this road (in June, 1883) I found a nest of the yellow-bellied flycatcher (Empidonax flaviventris). It was built at the base of a decayed stump, in a little depression between two roots, and was partially overarched with growing moss. It contained four eggs,—white, spotted with brown. I called upon the bird half a dozen times or more, and found her a model "keeper at home." On one occasion she allowed my hand to come within two or three inches of her bill. In every case she flew off without any outcry or ruse, and once at least she fell immediately to fly-catching with admirable philosophy. So far as I know, this is the only nest of the species ever found in New England outside of Maine. But it is proper to add that I did not capture the bird.

her bower with shells and other ornaments, why may not our little Northern darling beautify her nest with such humbler materials as her surroundings offer? On reflection, I am more and more convinced that the birds knew what they were doing; probably the female the moment she discovered the moss, called to her mate, "Oh, look, how lovely! Do, my dear, let's line our nest with it!"

This artistic structure was found on the anniversary of the battle of Bunker Hill, a day which I had been celebrating, as best I could, by climbing the highest hill in New England. Plunging into the woods within fifty yards of the Crawford House, I had gone up and up and on and on, through a magnificent forest, and then over more magnificent rocky heights, until I stood at last on the platform of the hotel at the summit. True, the path, which I had never traveled before, was wet and slippery, with stretches of ice and snow here and there; but the shifting view was so grand, the atmosphere so bracing, and the solitude so impressive that I enjoyed every step, till it came to clambering up the Mount Washington cone over the bowlders. At this point, to speak frankly, I began to hope that the ninth mile would prove to be a short one. The guide-books are agreed in warning the visitor against making this ascent without a companion, and no doubt they are right in so doing. A crippling accident would almost inevitably be fatal, while for several miles the trail is so indistinct that it would be difficult, if not impossible, to follow it in a fog. And yet, if one is willing to take the risk (and is not so unfortunate as never to have learned how to keep himself company), he will find a very considerable compensation in the peculiar pleasure to be experienced in being absolutely alone above the world. For myself, I was shut up to going in this way or not going at all; and a Bostonian must do something patriotic on the Seventeenth of June. But for all that, if the storm which chased me down the mountains in the afternoon, clouding first Mount Washington and then Mount Pleasant behind me, and shutting me in-doors all the next day, had started an hour sooner, or if I had been detained an hour later, it is not impossible that I might now be writing in a different strain.

My reception at the top was none of the heartiest. The hotel was tightly closed, while a large snow-bank stood guard before the door. However, I invited myself into the Signal Service Station, and made my wants known to one of the officers, who very kindly spread a table with such things as he and his companions had just been eating. It would be out of place to say much about the luncheon: the bread and butter were good, and the pudding was interesting. I had the cook's word for it that the latter was made of corn-starch, but he volunteered no explanation of its color, which was nearly that of chocolate. As a working hypothesis I adopted the molasses or brown-sugar theory, but a brief experiment (as brief as politeness permitted) indicated a total absence of any saccharine principle. But then, what do we climb mountains for, if not to see something out of the common course? On the whole, if this department of our national government is ever on trial for extravagance in the matter of high living, I shall be moved to offer myself as a competent witness for the defense.

A company of chimney-swifts were flying criss-cross over the summit, and one of the men said that he presumed they lived there. I took the liberty to doubt his opinion, however. To me it seemed nothing but a blunder that they should be there even for an hour. There could hardly be many insects at that height, I thought, and I had abundant cause to know that the woods below were full of them. I knew, also, that the swifts knew it; for while I had been prowling about between Crawford's and Fabyan's, they had several times shot by my head so closely that I had instinctively fallen to calculating the probable consequences of a collision. But, after all, the swift is no doubt a far better entomologist than I am, though he has never heard of Packard's Guide. Possibly there are certain species of insects, and those of a peculiarly delicate savor, which are to be obtained only at about this altitude.

The most enjoyable part of the Crawford path is the five miles from the top of Mount Clinton to the foot of the Mount Washington cone. Along this ridge I was delighted to find in blossom two beautiful Alpine plants, which I had missed in previous (July) visits,—the diapensia (Diapensia Lapponica) and the Lapland rose- bay (Rhododendron Lapponicum),—and to get also a single forward specimen of Potentilla frigida. Here and there was a humblebee, gathering honey from the small purple catkins of the prostrate willows, now in full bloom. (Rather high-minded humblebees, they seemed, more than five thousand feet above the sea!) Professional entomologists (the chimney-swift, perhaps, included) may smile at my simplicity, but I was surprised to find this "animated torrid zone," this "insect lover of the sun," in such a

Greenland climate. Did he not know that his own poet had, described him as "hot midsummer's petted crone"? But possibly he was equally surprised at my appearance. He might even have taken his turn at quoting Emerson:—

"Pants up hither the spruce clerk

From South Cove and City Wharf"?[13]

Of the two, he was unquestionably the more at home, for he was living where in forty-eight hours I should have found my death. So much is Bombus better than a man.

In a little pool of water, which seemed to be nothing but a transient puddle caused by the melting snow, was a tiny fish. I asked him by what miracle he got there, but he could give no explanation. He, too, might well enough have joined the noble company of Emersonians:—

"I never thought to ask, I never knew;

But, in my simple ignorance, suppose

The self-same Power that brought me here brought you."

Almost at the very top of Mount Clinton I was saluted by the familiar ditty of the Nashville warbler. I could hardly believe my ears; but there was no mistake, for the bird soon appeared in plain sight. Had it been one of the hardier-seeming species, the yellow-rumped for example, I should not have thought it very strange; but this dainty Helminthophaga, so common in the vicinity of Boston, did appear to be out of his latitude, summering here on Alpine heights. With a good pair of wings, and the whole continent to choose from, he surely might have found some more congenial spot than this in which to bring up his little family. I took his presence to be only an individual freak, but a subsequent visitor, who made the ascent from the Glen, reported the same species on that side also, and at about the same height.

These signs of life on bleak mountain ridges are highly interesting and suggestive. The fish, the humblebees, the birds, and a mouse which scampered away to its hole amid the rocks,—all these might have found

13. But by this time the clerk's appearance was, to say the least, not reprehensibly "spruce." For one thing, what with the moisture and the sharp stones, he was already becoming jealous of his shoes, lest they should not hold together till he could get back to the Crawford House.

better living elsewhere. But Nature will have her world full. Stunted life is better than none, she thinks. So she plants her forests of spruces, and keeps them growing, where, with all their efforts, they cannot get above the height of a man's knee. There is no beauty about them, no grace. They sacrifice symmetry and everything else for the sake of bare existence, reminding one of Satan's remark, "All that a man hath will he give for his life."

Very admirable are the devices by which vegetation maintains itself against odds. Everybody notices that many of the mountain species, like the diapensia, the rose-bay, the Greenland sandwort (called the mountain daisy by the Summit House people, for some inscrutable reason), and the phyllodoce, have blossoms disproportionately large and handsome; as if they realized that, in order to attract their indispensable allies, the insects, to these inhospitable regions, they must offer them some special inducements. Their case is not unlike that of a certain mountain hotel which might be named, which happens to be poorly situated, but which keeps itself full, nevertheless, by the peculiar excellence of its cuisine.

It does not require much imagination to believe that these hardy vegetable mountaineers love their wild, desolate dwelling-places as truly as do the human residents of the region. An old man in Bethlehem told me that sometimes, during the long, cold winter, he felt that perhaps it would be well for him, now his work was done, to sell his "place" and go down to Boston to live, near his brother. "But then," he added, "you know it's dangerous transplanting an old tree; you're likely as not to kill it." Whatever we have, in this world, we must pay for with the loss of something else. The bitter must be taken with the sweet, be we plants, animals, or men. These thoughts recurred to me a day or two later, as I lay on the summit of Mount Agassiz, in the sun and out of the wind, gazing down into the Franconia Valley, then in all its June beauty. Nestled under the lee of the mountain, but farther from the base, doubtless, than it seemed from my point of view, was a small dwelling, scarcely better than a shanty. Two or three young children were playing about the door, and near them was the man of the house splitting wood. The air was still enough for me to hear every blow, although it reached me only as the axe was again over the man's head, ready for the next descent. It was a charming picture,—the broad, green valley full of sunshine and peace, and the solitary cottage, from whose doorstep might be seen in one direction the noble Mount Washington range, and in another the hardly less noble Franconias. How easy to live simply and well in such a grand seclusion! But soon there came a thought of Wordsworth's sonnet, addressed to just such a mood, "Yes, there is holy pleasure in thine eye," and I felt at once the truth of his admonition. What if the cottage really were mine,—mine to spend a lifetime in? How quickly the poetry would turn to prose!

An hour afterwards, on my way back to the Sinclair House, I passed a group of men at work on the highway. One of them was a little apart from the rest, and out of a social impulse I accosted him with the remark, "I suppose, in heaven, the streets never will need mending." Quick as thought came the reply: "Well, I hope not. If I ever get there, I don't want to work on the road." Here spoke universal human nature, which finds its strong argument for immortality in its discontent with matters as they now are. The one thing we are all sure of is that we were born for something better than our present employment; and even those who school themselves most religiously in the virtue of contentment know very well how to define that grace so as not to exclude from it a comfortable mixture of "divine dissatisfaction." Well for us if we are still able to stand in our place and do faithfully our allotted task, like the mountain spruces and the Bethlehemite road-mender.

PHILLIDA AND CORIDON.

Fierce warres and faithful loves shall moralize my song.

— Spenser.

Much ado there was, God wot:
He would love, and she would not.

— Nicholas Breton.

PHILLIDA AND CORIDON.

The happiness of birds, heretofore taken for granted, and long ago put to service in a proverb, is in these last days made a matter of doubt. It transpires that they are engaged without respite in a struggle for existence,—a struggle so fierce that at least two of them perish every year for one that survives.[14] How, then, can they be otherwise than miserable?

There is no denying the struggle, of course; nor need we question some real effect produced by it upon the cheerfulness of the participants. The more rationalistic of the smaller species, we may be sure, find it hard to reconcile the existence of hawks and owls with the doctrine of an all-wise Providence; while even the most simple-minded of them can scarcely fail to realize that a world in which one is liable any day to be pursued by a boy with a shot-gun is not in any strict sense paradisiacal.

And yet, who knows the heart of a bird? A child, possibly, or a poet; certainly not a philosopher. And happiness, too,—is that something of which the scientific mind can render us a quite adequate description? Or is it, rather, a wayward, mysterious thing, coming often when least expected, and going away again when, by all tokens, it ought to remain? How is it with ourselves? Do we wait to weigh all the good and evil of our state, to take an accurate account of it pro and con, before we allow ourselves to be glad or sorry? Not many of us, I think. Mortuary tables

14. Wallace, Natural Selection, p. 30.

may demonstrate that half the children born in this country fail to reach the age of twenty years. But what then? Our "expectation of life" is not based upon statistics. The tables may be correct, for aught we know; but they deal with men in general and on the average; they have no message for you and me individually. And it seems not unlikely that birds may be equally illogical; always expecting to live, and not die, and often giving themselves up to impulses of gladness without stopping to inquire whether, on grounds of absolute reason, these impulses are to be justified. Let us hope so, at all events, till somebody proves the contrary.

But even looking at the subject a little more philosophically, we may say—and be thankful to say it—that the joy of life is not dependent upon comfort, nor yet upon safety. The essential matter is that the heart be engaged. Then, though we be toiling up the Matterhorn, or swept along in the rush of a bayonet charge, we may still find existence not only endurable, but in the highest degree exhilarating. On the other hand, if there is no longer anything we care for; if enthusiasm is dead, and hope also, then, though we have all that money can buy, suicide is perhaps the only fitting action that is left for us,—unless, perchance, we are still able to pass the time in writing treatises to prove that everybody else ought to be as unhappy as ourselves.

Birds have many enemies and their full share of privation, but I do not believe that they often suffer from ennui. Having "neither storehouse nor barn,"[15] they are never in want of something to do. From sunrise till noon there is the getting of breakfast, then from noon till sunset the getting of dinner,—both out-of-doors, and without any trouble of cookery or dishes,—a kind of perpetual picnic. What could be simpler or more delightful? Carried on in this way, eating is no longer the coarse and sensual thing we make it, with our set meal-times and elaborate preparations.

---

15. The shrike lays up grasshoppers and sparrows, and the California woodpecker hoards great numbers of acorns, but it is still in dispute, I believe, whether thrift is the motive with either of them. Considering what has often been done in similar cases, we may think it surprising that the Scripture text above quoted (together with its exegetical parallel, Matthew vi. 26) has never been brought into court to settle the controversy; but to the best of my knowledge it never has been.

Country children know that there are two ways to go berrying. According to the first of these you stroll into the pasture in the cool of the day, and at your leisure pick as many as you choose of the ripest and largest of the berries, putting every one into your mouth. This is agreeable. According to the second, you carry a basket, which you are expected to bring home again well filled. And this method—well, tastes will differ, but following the good old rule for judging in such cases, I must believe that most unsophisticated persons prefer the other. The hand-to-mouth process certainly agrees best with our idea of life in Eden; and, what is more to the purpose now, it is the one which the birds, still keeping the garden instead of tilling the ground, continue to follow.

That this unworldliness of the birds has any religious or theological significance I do not myself suppose. Still, as anybody may see, there are certain very plain Scripture texts on their side. Indeed, if birds were only acute theologians, they would unquestionably proceed to turn these texts (since they find it so easy to obey them) into the basis of a "system of truth." Other parts of the Bible must be interpreted, to be sure (so the theory would run); but these statements mean just what they say, and whoever meddles with them is carnally minded and a rationalist.

Somebody will object, perhaps, that, with our talk about a "perpetual picnic," we are making a bird's life one cloudless holiday; contradicting what we have before admitted about a struggle for existence, and leaving out of sight altogether the seasons of scarcity, the storms, and the biting cold. But we intend no such foolish recantation. These hardships are real enough, and serious enough. What we maintain is that evils of this kind are not necessarily inconsistent with enjoyment, and may even give to life an additional zest. It is a matter of every-day observation that the people who have nothing to do except to "live well" (as the common sarcasm has it) are not always the most cheerful; while there are certain diseases, like pessimism and the gout, which seem appointed to wait on luxury and idleness,—as though nature were determined to have the scales kept somewhat even. And surely this divine law of compensation has not left the innocent birds unprovided for,—the innocent birds of whom it was said, "Your heavenly Father feedeth them." How must the devoted pair exult, when, in spite of owls and hawks, squirrels and weasels, small boys and full-grown oölogists, they have finally reared a brood of offspring! The long uncertainty and the thousand perils only intensify the joy. In truth, so far as this world is concerned, the highest bliss is never to be had without antecedent sorrow; and even of heaven itself we may not scruple to say that, if there are painters there, they probably feel obliged to put some shadows into their pictures.

But of course (and this is what we have been coming to through this long introduction),—of course our friends of the air are happiest in the season of mating; happiest, and therefore most attractive to us who find our pleasure in studying them. In spring, of all times of the year, it seems a pity that everybody should not turn ornithologist. For "all mankind love a lover;" and the world, in consequence, has given itself up to novel-reading, not knowing, unfortunately, how much better that rôle is taken by the birds than by the common run of story-book heroes.

People whose notions of the subject are derived from attending to the antics of our imported sparrows have no idea how delicate and beautiful a thing a real feathered courtship is. To tell the truth, these foreigners have associated too long and too intimately with men, and have fallen far away from their primal innocence. There is no need to describe their actions. The vociferous and most unmannerly importunity of the suitor, and the correspondingly spiteful rejection of his overtures by the little vixen on whom his affections are for the moment placed,—these we have all seen to our hearts' discontent.

The sparrow will not have been brought over the sea for nothing, however, if his bad behavior serves to heighten our appreciation of our own native songsters, with their "perfect virtues" and "manners for the heart's delight."

The American robin, for instance, is far from being a bird of exceptional refinement. His nest is rude, not to say slovenly, and his general deportment is unmistakably common. But watch him when he goes a-wooing, and you will begin to feel quite a new respect for him. How gently he approaches his beloved! How carefully he avoids ever coming disrespectfully near! No sparrow-like screaming, no dancing about, no melodramatic gesticulation. If she moves from one side of the tree to the other, or to the tree adjoining, he follows in silence. Yet every movement is a petition, an assurance that his heart is hers and ever must be. The action is extremely simple; there is nothing of which to make an eloquent description; but I should pity the man who could witness it with indifference. Not that the robin's suit is always carried on in the same way; he is much too versatile for that. On one occasion, at least, I saw him holding himself absolutely motionless, in a horizontal posture, staring at his sweetheart as if he would charm her with his gaze, and emitting all the while a subdued hissing sound. The significance of this conduct I do not profess to have understood; it ended with his suddenly darting at the female, who took wing and was pursued. Not improbably the robin finds the feminine nature somewhat fickle, and counts it expedient to vary his tactics accordingly; for it is getting to be more and more believed that, in kind at least, the intelligence of the lower animals is not different from ours.

I once came unexpectedly upon a wood thrush, who was in the midst of a performance very similar to this of the robin standing on the dead branch of a tree, with his crown feathers erect, his bill set wide open, and his whole body looking as rigid as death. His mate, as I perceived the next moment, was not far away, on the same limb. If he was attempting fascination, he had gone very clumsily about it, I thought, unless his mate's idea of beauty was totally different from mine; for I could hardly keep from laughing at his absurd appearance. It did not occur to me till afterwards that he had perhaps heard of Othello's method, and was at that moment acting out a story

"of most disastrous chances,
Of moving accidents by flood and field,
Of hair-breadth scapes i' the imminent deadly breach,
Of being taken by the insolent foe
And sold to slavery."

How much depends upon the point of view! Here was I, ready to laugh; while poor Desdemona only thought, "'Twas pitiful, 'twas wondrous pitiful." Dear sympathetic soul! Let us hope that she was never called to play out the tragedy.

Two things are very noticeable during the pairing season,—the scarcity of females and their indifference. Every one of them seems to have at least two admirers dangling after her,[16] while she is almost sure

16. So near do birds come to Mr. Ruskin's idea that "a girl worth anything ought to have always half a dozen or so of suitors under vow for her."

to carry herself as if a wedding were the last thing she would ever consent to think of; and that not because of bashfulness, but from downright aversion. The observer begins to suspect that the fair creatures have really entered into some sort of no-marriage league, and that there are not to be any nests this year, nor any young birds. But by and by he discovers that somehow, he cannot surmise how,—it must have been when his eyes were turned the other way,—the scene is entirely changed, the maidens are all wedded, and even now the nests are being got ready.

I watched a trio of cat-birds in a clump of alder bushes by the roadside; two males, almost as a matter of course, "paying attentions" to one female. Both suitors were evidently in earnest; each hoped to carry off the prize, and perhaps felt that he should be miserable forever if he were disappointed; and yet, on their part, everything was being done decently and in order. So far as I saw, there was no disposition to quarrel. Only let the dear creature choose one of them, and the other would take his broken heart away. So, always at a modest remove, they followed her about from bush to bush, entreating her in most loving and persuasive tones to listen to their suit. But she, all this time, answered every approach with a snarl; she would never have anything to do with either of them; she disliked them both, and only wished they would leave her to herself. This lasted as long as I stayed to watch. Still I had little doubt she fully intended to accept one of them, and had even made up her mind already which it should be. She knew enough, I felt sure, to calculate the value of a proper maidenly reluctance. How could her mate be expected to rate her at her worth, if she allowed herself to be won too easily? Besides, she could afford not to be in haste, seeing she had a choice of two.

What a comfortably simple affair the matrimonial question is with the feminine cat-bird! Her wooers are all of equally good family and all equally rich. There is literally nothing for her to do but to look into her own heart and choose. No temptation has she to sell herself for the sake of a fashionable name or a fine house, or in order to gratify the prejudice of father or mother. As for a marriage settlement, she knows neither the name nor the thing. In fact, marriage in her thought is a simple union of hearts, with no taint of anything mercantile about it. Happy cat-bird! She perhaps imagines that human marriages are of the same ideal sort!

I have spoken of the affectionate language of these dusky lovers; but it was noticeable that they did not sing, although, to have fulfilled the common idea of such an affair, they certainly should have been doing so, and each trying his best to outsing the other. Possibly there had already been such a tournament before my arrival; or, for aught I know, this particular female may have given out that she had no ear for music.

In point of fact, however, there was nothing peculiar in their conduct. No doubt, in the earlier stages of a bird's attachment he is likely to express his passion musically; but later he is not content to warble from a tree-top. There are things to be said which cannot appropriately be spoken at long range; and unless my study of novels has been to little purpose, all this agrees well with the practices of human gallants. Do not these begin by singing under the lady's window, or by sending verses to her? and are not such proceedings intended to prepare the way, as speedily as possible, for others of a more satisfying, though it may be of a less romantic nature?

Bearing this in mind, we may be able to account, in part at least, for the inexperienced observer's disappointment when, fresh from the perusal of (for example) the thirteenth chapter of Darwin's "Descent of Man," he goes into the woods to look about for himself. He expects to find here and there two or three songsters, each in turn doing his utmost to surpass the brilliancy and power of the other's music; while a feminine auditor sits in full view, preparing to render her verdict, and reward the successful competitor with her own precious self. This would be a pretty picture. Unfortunately, it is looked for in vain. The two or three singers may be found, likely enough; but the female, if she be indeed within hearing, is modestly hidden away somewhere in the bushes, and our student is none the wiser. Let him watch as long as he please, he will hardly see the prize awarded.

Nevertheless he need not grudge the time thus employed; not, at any rate, if he be sensitive to music. For it will be found that birds have at least one attribute of genius: they can do their best only on great occasions. Our brown thrush, for instance, is a magnificent singer, albeit he is not of the best school, being too "sensational" to suit the most exacting taste. His song is a grand improvisation: a good deal jumbled, to be sure, and without any recognizable form or theme; and yet, like a Liszt rhapsody, it perfectly answers its purpose,—that is, it gives the performer full scope to show what he can do with his instrument. You may laugh a little, if you like, at an occasional grotesque or overwrought passage, but unless you are well used to it you will surely be astonished. Such power and range of voice; such startling transitions; such endless variety! And withal such boundless enthusiasm and almost incredible endurance! Regarded as pure music, one strain of the hermit thrush is to my mind worth the whole of it; just as a single movement of Beethoven's is better than a world of Liszt transcriptions. But in its own way it is unsurpassable.

Still, though this is a meagre and quite unexaggerated account of the ordinary song of the brown thrush, I have discovered that even he can be outdone—by himself. One morning in early May I came upon three birds of this species, all singing at once, in a kind of jealous frenzy. As they sang they continually shifted from tree to tree, and one in particular (the one nearest to where I stood) could hardly be quiet a moment. Once he sang with full power while on the ground (or close to it, for he was just then behind a low bush), after which he mounted to the very tip of a tall pine, which bent beneath his weight. In the midst of the hurly-burly one of the trio suddenly sounded the whip-poor-will's call twice,—an absolutely perfect reproduction.[17]

The significance of all this sound and fury,—what the prize was, if any, and who obtained it,—this another can conjecture as well as myself. I know no more than old Kaspar:——

"'Why, that I cannot tell,' said he,

But 'twas a famous victory.'"

As I turned to come away, the contest all at once ceased, and the silence of the woods, or what seemed like silence, was really impressive. The chewinks and field sparrows were singing, but it was like the music of a village singer after Patti; or, to make the comparison less unjust, like the Pastoral Symphony of Handel after a Wagner tempest.

---

17. "That's the wise thrush: he sings each song twice over,

Lest you should think he never could recapture

The first fine careless rapture!"

The "authorities" long since forbade Harporhynchus rufus to play the mimic. Probably in the excitement of the moment this fellow forgot himself.

It is curious how deeply we are sometimes affected by a very trifling occurrence. I have remembered many times a slight scene in which three purple finches were the actors. Of the two males, one was in full adult plumage of bright crimson, while the other still wore his youthful suit of brown. First, the older bird suspended himself in mid air, and sang most beautifully; dropping, as he concluded, to a perch beside the female. Then the younger candidate, who was already sitting near by, took his turn, singing nearly or quite as well as his rival, but without quitting the branch, though his wings quivered. I saw no more. Yet, as I say, I have often since thought of the three birds, and wondered whether the bright feathers and the flying song carried the day against the younger suitor. I fear they did. Sometimes, too, I have queried whether young birds (who none the less are of age to marry) can be so very meek or so very dull as never to rebel against the fashion that only the old fellows shall dress handsomely; and I have tried in vain to imagine the mutterings, deep and loud, which such a law would excite in certain other quarters. It pains me to say it, but I suspect that taxation without representation would seem a small injustice, in comparison.

Like these linnets in the exceptional interest they excited were two large seabirds, who suddenly appeared circling about over the woods, as I was taking a solitary walk on a Sunday morning in April. One of them was closely pursuing the other; not as though he were trying to overtake her, but rather as though he were determined to keep her company. They swept now this way, now that,—now lost to sight, and now reappearing; and once they passed straight over my head, so that I heard the whistling of their wings. Then they were off, and I saw them no more. They came from far, and by night they were perhaps a hundred leagues away. But I followed them with my blessing, and to this day I feel toward them a little as I suppose we all do toward a certain few strangers whom we have met here and there in our journeyings, and chatted with for an hour or two. We had never seen them before; if we learned their names we have long ago forgotten them; but somehow the persons themselves keep a place in our memory, and even in our affection.

"I crossed a moor, with a name of its own

And a certain use in the world, no doubt;

Yet a hand's breadth of it shines alone

'Mid the blank miles round about:

"For there I picked up on the heather,

And there I put inside my breast,

A moulted feather, an eagle-feather!

Well, I forget the rest."

Since we cannot ask birds for an explanation of their conduct, we have nothing for it but to steal their secrets, as far as possible, by patient and stealthy watching. In this way I hope, sooner or later, to find out what the golden-winged woodpecker means by the shout with which he makes the fields reëcho in the spring, especially in the latter half of April. I have no doubt it has something to do with the process of mating, but it puzzles me to guess just what the message can be which requires to be published so loudly. Such a stentorian, long-winded cry! You wonder where the bird finds breath for such an effort, and think he must be a very ungentle lover, surely. But withhold your judgment for a few days, till you see him and his mate gamboling about the branches of some old tree, calling in soft, affectionate tones, Wick-a-wick, wick-a-wick; then you will confess that, whatever failings the golden-wing may have, he is not to be charged with insensibility. The fact is that our "yellow-hammer" has a genius for noise. When he is very happy he drums. Sometimes, indeed, he marvels how birds who haven't this resource are able to get through the world at all. Nor ought we to think it strange if in his love-making he finds great use for this his crowning accomplishment. True, we have nowhere read of a human lover's serenading his mistress with a drum; but we must remember what creatures of convention men are, and that there is no inherent reason why a drum should not serve as well as a flute for such a purpose.

"All thoughts, all passions, all delights,

Whatever stirs this mortal frame,

All are but ministers of Love,

And feed his sacred flame."

I saw two of these flickers clinging to the trunk of a shell-bark tree; which, by the way, is a tree after the woodpecker's own heart. One was perhaps fifteen feet above the other, and before each was a strip of loose bark, a sort of natural drum-head. First, the lower one "beat his music out," rather softly. Then, as he ceased, and held his head back to listen, the other answered him; and so the dialogue went on. Evidently, they were already mated, and were now renewing their mutual vows; for birds, to their praise be it spoken, believe in courtship after marriage. The day happened to be Sunday, and it did occur to me that possibly this was the woodpeckers' ritual,—a kind of High Church service, with antiphonal choirs. But I dismissed the thought; for, on the whole, the shouting seems more likely to be diagnostic, and in spite of his gold-lined wings, I have set the flicker down as almost certainly an old-fashioned Methodist.

Speaking of courtship after marriage, I am reminded of a spotted sandpiper, whose capers I amused myself with watching, one day last June, on the shore of Saco Lake. As I caught sight of him, he was straightening himself up, with a pretty, self-conscious air, at the same time spreading his white-edged tail, and calling, Tweet, tweet, tweet. [18] Afterwards he got upon a log, where, with head erect and wings thrown forward and downward, he ran for a yard or two, calling as before. This trick seemed especially to please him, and was several times repeated. He ran rapidly, and with a comical prancing movement; but nothing he did was half so laughable as the behavior of his mate, who all this while dressed her feathers without once deigning to look at her spouse's performance. Undoubtedly they had been married for several weeks, and she was, by this time, well used to his nonsense. It must be a devoted husband, I fancy, who continues to offer attentions when they are received in such a spirit.

Walking a log is a somewhat common practice with birds. I once detected our little golden-crowned thrush showing off in this way to his mate, who stood on the ground close at hand. In his case the head was lowered instead of raised, and the general effect was heightened by his curiously precise gait, which even on ordinary occasions is enough to provoke a smile.

---

18. May one who knows nothing of philology venture to inquire whether the very close agreement of this tweet with our sweet (compare also the Anglo-Saxon swéte, the Icelandic sœtr, and the Sanskrit svad) does not point to a common origin of the Aryan and sandpiper languages?

Not improbably every species of birds has its own code of etiquette; unwritten, of course, but carefully handed down from father to son, and faithfully observed. Nor is it cause for wonder if, in our ignorant eyes, some of these "society manners" look a little ridiculous. Even the usages of fashionable human circles have not always escaped the laughter of the profane.

I was standing on the edge of a small thicket, observing a pair of cuckoos as they made a break fast out of a nest of tent caterpillars (it was a feast rather than a common meal; for the caterpillars were plentiful, and, as I judged, just at their best, being about half grown), when a couple of scarlet tanagers appeared upon the scene. The female presently selected a fine strip of cedar bark, and started off with it, sounding a call to her handsome husband, who at once followed in her wake. I thought, What a brute, to leave his wife to build the house! But he, plainly enough, felt that in escorting her back and forth he was doing all that ought to be expected of any well-bred, scarlet-coated tanager. And the lady herself, if one might infer anything from her tone and demeanor, was of the same opinion. I mention this trifling occurrence, not to put any slight upon Pyranga rubra (who am I, that I should accuse so gentle and well dressed a bird of bad manners?), but merely as an example of the way in which feathered politeness varies. In fact, it seems not unlikely that the male tanager may abstain on principle from taking any active part in constructing the nest, lest his fiery color should betray its whereabouts. As for his kindness and loyalty, I only wish I could feel as sure of one half the human husbands whom I meet.

It would be very ungallant of me, however, to leave my readers to understand that the female bird is always so unsympathetic as most of the descriptions thus far given would appear to indicate. In my memory are several scenes, any one of which, if I could put it on paper as I saw it, would suffice to correct such an erroneous impression. In one of these the parties were a pair of chipping sparrows. Never was man so churlish that his heart would not have been touched with the vision of their gentle but rapturous delight. As they chased each other gayly from branch to branch and from tree to tree, they flew with that delicate, affected movement of the wings which birds are accustomed to use at such times, and which, perhaps, bears the same relation to their ordinary flight that dancing does to the every-day walk of men and women. The two seemed equally enchanted, and both sang. Little they knew of the "struggle for existence" and the "survival of the fittest." Adam and Eve, in Paradise, were never more happy.

A few weeks later, taking an evening walk, I was stopped by the sight of a pair of cedar-birds on a stone wall. They had chosen a convenient flat stone, and were hopping about upon it, pausing every moment or two to put their little bills together. What a loving ecstasy possessed them! Sometimes one, sometimes the other, sounded a faint lisping note, and motioned for another kiss. But there is no setting forth the ineffable grace and sweetness of their chaste behavior. I looked and looked, till a passing carriage frightened them away. They were only common cedar-birds; if I were to see them again I should not know them; but if my pen were equal to my wish, they should be made immortal.

SCRAPING ACQUAINTANCE.

A man that hath friends must show himself friendly.

— Proverbs xviii. 24.

SCRAPING ACQUAINTANCE.

As I was crossing Boston Common, some years ago, my attention was caught by the unusual behavior of a robin, who was standing on the lawn, absolutely motionless, and every few seconds making a faint hissing noise. So much engaged was he that, even when a dog ran near him, he only started slightly, and on the instant resumed his statue-like attitude. Wondering what this could mean, and not knowing how else to satisfy my curiosity, I bethought myself of a man whose letters about birds I had now and then noticed in the daily press. So, looking up his name in the City Directory, and finding that he lived at such a number, Beacon Street, I wrote him a note of inquiry. He must have been amused as he read it; for I remember giving him the title of "Esquire," and speaking of his communications to the newspapers as the ground of my application to him. "Such is fame!" he likely enough said to himself. "Here is a man with eyes in his head, a man, moreover, who has probably been at school in his time,—for most of his words are spelled correctly,—and yet he knows my name only as he has seen it signed once in a while to a few lines in a newspaper." Thoughts like these, however, did not prevent his replying to the note (my "valued favor") with all politeness, although he confessed himself unable to answer my question; and by the time I had occasion to trouble him again I had learned that he was to be addressed as Doctor, and, furthermore, was an ornithologist of world-wide reputation, being, in fact, one of the three joint-authors of the most important work so far issued on the birds of North America.

Certainly I was and am grateful to him (he is now dead) for his generous treatment of my ignorance; but even warmer is my feeling toward that city thrush, who, all unconscious of what he was doing, started me that day on a line of study which has been ever since a continual delight. Most gladly would I do him any kindness in my power; but I have little doubt that, long ere this, he, too, has gone the way of all the earth. As to what he was thinking about on that memorable May morning, I am as much in the dark as ever. But there is no law against a bird's behaving mysteriously, I suppose. Most of us, I am sure, often do things which are inexplicable to ourselves, and once in a very great while, perhaps, it would puzzle even our next-door neighbors to render a complete account of our motives.

Whatever the robin meant, however, and no doubt there was some good reason for his conduct, he had given my curiosity the needed jog. Now, at last, I would do what I had often dreamed of doing,—learn something about the birds of my own region, and be able to recognize at least the more common ones when I saw them.

The interest of the study proved to be the greater for my ignorance, which, to speak within bounds, was nothing short of wonderful; perhaps I might appropriately use a more fashionable word, and call it phenomenal. All my life long I had had a kind of passion for being out-of-doors; and, to tell the truth, I had been so often seen wandering by myself in out-of-the-way wood-paths, or sitting idly about on stone walls in lonesome pastures, that some of my Philistine townsmen had most likely come to look upon me as no better than a vagabond. Yet I was not a vagabond, for all that. I liked work, perhaps, as well as the generality of people. But I was unfortunate in this respect: while I enjoyed in-door work, I hated to be in the house; and, on the other hand, while I enjoyed being out-of-doors, I hated all manner of out-door employment. I was not lazy, but I possessed—well, let us call it the true aboriginal temperament; though I fear that this distinction will be found too subtile, even for the well-educated, unless, along with their education, they have a certain sympathetic bias, which, after all, is the main thing to be depended on in such nice psychological discriminations.

With all my rovings in wood and field, however, I knew nothing of any open-air study. Study was a thing of books. At school we were never taught to look elsewhere for knowledge. Reading and spelling, geography and grammar, arithmetic and algebra, geometry and trigonometry,—these were studied, of course, as also were Latin and

Greek. But none of our lessons took us out of the school-room, unless it was astronomy, the study of which I had nearly forgotten; and that we pursued in the night-time, when birds and plants were as though they were not. I cannot recollect that any one of my teachers ever called my attention to a natural object. It seems incredible, but, so far as my memory serves, I was never in the habit of observing the return of the birds in the spring or their departure in the autumn; except, to be sure, that the semi-annual flight of the ducks and geese was always a pleasant excitement, more especially because there were several lakes (invariably spoken of as ponds) in our vicinity, on the borders of which the village "gunners" built pine-branch booths in the season.

But now, as I have said, my ignorance was converted all at once into a kind of blessing; for no sooner had I begun to read bird books, and consult a cabinet of mounted specimens, than every turn out-of-doors became full of all manner of delightful surprises. Could it be that what I now beheld with so much wonder was only the same as had been going on year after year in these my own familiar lanes and woods? Truly the human eye is nothing more than a window, of no use unless the man looks out of it.

Some of the experiences of that period seem ludicrous enough in the retrospect. Only two or three days after my eyes were first opened I was out with a friend in search of wild-flowers (I was piloting him to a favorite station for Viola pubescens), when I saw a most elegant little creature, mainly black and white, but with brilliant orange markings. He was darting hither and thither among the branches of some low trees, while I stared at him in amazement, calling on my comrade, who was as ignorant as myself, but less excited, to behold the prodigy. Half trembling lest the bird should prove to be some straggler from the tropics, the like of which would not be found in the cabinet before mentioned, I went thither that very evening. Alas, my silly fears! there stood the little beauty's exact counterpart, labeled Setophaga ruticilla, the American redstart,—a bird which the manual assured me was very common in my neighborhood.

But it was not my eyes only that were opened, my ears also were touched. It was as if all the birds had heretofore been silent, and now, under some sudden impulse, had broken out in universal concert. What a glorious chorus it was; and every voice a stranger! For a week or more I was puzzled by a song which I heard without fail whenever I went into the woods, but the author of which I could never set eyes on,—a song so exceptionally loud and shrill, and marked by such a vehement crescendo, that, even to my new-found ears, it stood out from the general medley a thing by itself. Many times I struck into the woods in the direction whence it came, but without getting so much as a flying glimpse of the musician. Very mysterious, surely! Finally, by accident I believe, I caught the fellow in the very act of singing, as he stood on a dead pine-limb; and a few minutes later he was on the ground, walking about (not hopping) with the primmest possible gait,—a small olive-brown bird, with an orange crown and a speckled breast. Then I knew him for the golden-crowned thrush; but it was not for some time after this that I heard his famous evening song, and it was longer still before I found his curious roofed nest.

"Happy those early days," those days of childish innocence,—though I was a man grown,—when every bird seemed newly created, and even the redstart and the wood wagtail were like rarities from the ends of the earth. Verily, my case was like unto Adam's, when every fowl of the air was brought before him for a name.

One evening, on my way back to the city after an afternoon ramble, I stopped just at dusk in a grove of hemlocks, and soon out of the tree-top overhead came a song,—a brief strain of about six notes, in a musical but rather rough voice, and in exquisite accord with the quiet solemnity of the hour. Again and again the sounds fell on my ear, and as often I endeavored to obtain a view of the singer; but he was in the thick of the upper branches, and I looked for him in vain. How delicious the music was! a perfect lullaby, drowsy and restful; like the benediction of the wood on the spirit of a tired city-dweller. I blessed the unknown songster in return; and even now I have a feeling that the peculiar enjoyment which the song of the black-throated green warbler never fails to afford me may perhaps be due in some measure to its association with that twilight hour.

To this same hemlock grove I was in the habit, in those days, of going now and then to listen to the evening hymn of the veery, or Wilson thrush. Here, if nowhere else, might be heard music fit to be called sacred. Nor did it seem a disadvantage, but rather the contrary, when, as sometimes happened, I was compelled to take my seat in the edge of the wood, and wait quietly, in the gathering darkness, for vespers to begin. The veery's mood is not so lofty as the hermit's, nor is his music to be compared for brilliancy and fullness with that of the wood thrush; but, more than any other bird-song known to me, the veery's has, if I may say so, the accent of sanctity. Nothing is here of self-consciousness; nothing of earthly pride or passion. If we chance to overhear it and laud the singer, that is our affair. Simple-hearted worshiper that he is, he has never dreamed of winning praise for himself by the excellent manner in which he praises his Creator,—an absence of thrift, which is very becoming in thrushes, though, I suppose, it is hardly to be looked for in human choirs.

And yet, for all the unstudied ease and simplicity of the veery's strain, he is a great master of technique. In his own artless way he does what I have never heard any other bird attempt: he gives to his melody all the force of harmony. How this unique and curious effect, this vocal double-stopping, as a violinist might term it, is produced, is not certainly known; but it would seem that it must be by an arpeggio, struck with such consummate quickness and precision that the ear is unable to follow it, and is conscious of nothing but the resultant chord. At any rate, the thing itself is indisputable, and has often been commented on.

Moreover, this is only half the veery's technical proficiency. Once in a while, at least, he will favor you with a delightful feat of ventriloquism; beginning to sing in single voice, as usual, and anon, without any noticeable increase in the loudness of the tones, diffusing the music throughout the wood, as if there were a bird in every tree, all singing together in the strictest time. I am not sure that all members of the species possess this power, and I have never seen the performance alluded to in print; but I have heard it when the illusion was complete, and the effect most beautiful.

Music so devout and unostentatious as the veery's does not appeal to the hurried or the preoccupied. If you would enjoy it you must bring an ear to hear. I have sometimes pleased myself with imagining a resemblance between it and the poetry of George Herbert,—both uncared for by the world, but both, on that very account, prized all the more dearly by the few in every generation whose spirits are in tune with theirs.

This bird is one of a group of small thrushes called the Hylocichlæ, of which group we have five representatives in the Atlantic States: the wood thrush; the Wilson, or tawny thrush; the hermit; the olive-backed, or Swainson; and the gray-cheeked, or Alice's thrush. To the unpracticed eye the five all look alike. All of them, too, have the same glorious voice, so that the young student is pretty sure to find it a matter of some difficulty to tell them apart. Yet there are differences of coloration which may be trusted as constant, and to which, after a while, the eye becomes habituated; and, at the same time, each species has a song and call-notes peculiar to itself. One cannot help wishing, indeed, that he might hear the five singing by turns in the same wood. Then he could fix the distinguishing peculiarities of the different songs in his mind so as never to confuse them again. But this is more than can be hoped for; the listener must be content with hearing two, or at the most three, of the species singing together, and trust his memory to make the necessary comparison.

The song of the wood thrush is perhaps the most easily set apart from the rest, because of its greater compass of voice and bravery of execution. The Wilson's song, as you hear it by itself, seems so perfectly characteristic that you fancy you can never mistake any other for it; and yet, if you are in northern New England only a week afterwards, you may possibly hear a Swainson (especially if he happens to be one of the best singers of his species, and, more especially still, if he happens to be at just the right distance away), who you will say, at first thought, is surely a Wilson. The difficulty of distinguishing the voices is naturally greatest in the spring, when they have not been heard for eight or nine months. Here, as elsewhere, the student must be willing to learn the same lesson over and over, letting patience have her perfect work. That the five songs are really distinguishable is well illustrated by the fact (which I have before mentioned), that the presence of the Alice thrush in New England during the breeding season was announced as probable by myself, simply on the strength of a song which I had heard in the White Mountains, and which, as I believed, must be his, notwithstanding I was entirely unacquainted with it, and though all our books affirmed that the Alice thrush was not a summer resident of any part of the United States.

It is worth remarking, also, in this connection, that the Hylocichlæ differ more decidedly in their notes of alarm than in their songs. The wood thrush's call is extremely sharp and brusque, and is usually fired off in a little volley; that of the Wilson is a sort of whine, or snarl, in distressing contrast with his song; the hermit's is a quick, sotto voce, sometimes almost inaudible chuck; the Swainson's is a mellow whistle; while that of the Alice is something between the Swainson's and the Wilson's,—not so gentle and refined as the former, nor so outrageously vulgar as the latter.

In what is here said about discriminating species it must be understood that I am not speaking of such identification as will answer a strictly scientific purpose. For that the bird must be shot. To the maiden

"whose light blue eyes

Are tender over drowning flies,"

this decree will no doubt sound cruel. Men who pass laws of that sort may call themselves ornithologists, if they will; for her part she calls them butchers. We might turn on our fair accuser, it is true, with some inquiry about the two or three bird-skins which adorn her bonnet. But that would be only giving one more proof of our heartlessness; and, besides, unless a man is downright angry he can scarcely feel that he has really cleared himself when he has done nothing more than to point the finger and say, You're another. However, I am not set for the defence of ornithologists. They are abundantly able to take care of themselves without the help of any outsider. I only declare that, even to my unprofessional eye, this rule of theirs seems wise and necessary. They know, if their critics do not, how easy it is to be deceived; how many times things have been seen and minutely described, which, as was afterwards established, could not by any possibility have been visible. Moreover, regret it as we may, it is clear that in this world nobody can escape giving and taking more or less pain. We of the sterner sex are accustomed to think that even our blue-eyed censors are not entirely innocent in this regard; albeit, for myself, I am bound to believe that generally they are not to blame for the tortures they inflict upon us.

Granting the righteousness of the scientist's caution, however, we may still find a less rigorous code sufficient for our own non-scientific, though I hope not unscientific, purpose. For it is certain that no great enjoyment of bird study is possible for some of us, if we are never to be allowed to call our gentle friends by name until in every case we have gone through the formality of a post-mortem examination. Practically, and for every-day ends, we may know a robin, or a redstart, or even a hermit thrush, when we see him, without first turning the bird into a specimen.

Probably there are none of our birds which afford more surprise and pleasure to a novice than the family of warblers. A well-known ornithologist has related how one day he wandered into the forest in an idle mood, and accidentally catching a gleam of bright color overhead, raised his gun and brought the bird to his feet; and how excited and charmed he was with the wondrous beauty of his little trophy. Were there other birds in the woods as lovely as this? He would see for himself. And that was the beginning of what bids fair to prove a life-long enthusiasm.

Thirty-eight warblers are credited to New England; but it would be safe to say that not more than three of them are known to the average New-Englander. How should he know them, indeed? They do not come about the flower-garden like the humming-bird, nor about the lawn like the robin; neither can they be hunted with a dog like the grouse and the woodcock. Hence, for all their gorgeous apparel, they are mainly left to students and collectors. Of our common species the most beautiful are, perhaps, the blue yellow-back, the blue golden-wing, the Blackburnian, the black-and-yellow, the Canada flycatcher, and the redstart; with the yellow-rump, the black-throated green, the prairie warbler, the summer yellow-bird, and the Maryland yellow-throat coming not far behind. But all of them are beautiful, and they possess, besides, the charm of great diversity of plumage and habits; while some of them have the further merit, by no means inconsiderable, of being rare.

It was a bright day for me when the blue golden-winged warbler settled in my neighborhood. On my morning walk I detected a new song, and, following it up, found a new bird,—a result which is far from being a thing of course. The spring migration was at its height, and at first I expected to have the pleasure of my new friend's society for only a day or two; so I made the most of it. But it turned out that he and his companion had come to spend the summer, and before very long I discovered their nest. This was still unfinished when I came upon it; but I knew pretty well whose it was, having several times noticed the birds about the spot, and a few days after wards the female bravely sat still, while I bent over her, admiring her courage and her handsome dress. I paid my respects to the little mother almost daily, but jealously guarded her secret, sharing it only with a kind-hearted woman, whom I took with me on one of my visits. But, alas! one day I called, only to find the nest empty. Whether the villain who pillaged it traveled on two legs, or on four, I never knew. Possibly he dropped out of the air. But I wished him no good, whoever he was. Next year the birds appeared again, and more than one pair of them; but no nest could I find, though I often looked for it, and, as children say in their games, was sometimes very warm.

Is there any lover of birds in whose mind certain birds and certain places are not indissolubly joined? Most of us, I am sure, could go over the list and name the exact spots where we first saw this one, where we first heard that one sing, and where we found our first nest of the other. There is a piece of swampy woodland in Jefferson, New Hampshire, midway between the hotels and the railway station, which, for me, will always be associated with the song of the winter wren. I had been making an attempt to explore the wood, with a view to its botanical treasures, but the mosquitoes had rallied with such spirit that I was glad to beat a retreat to the road. Just then an unseen bird broke out into a song, and by the time he had finished I was saying to myself, A winter wren! Now, if I could only see him in the act, and so be sure of the correctness of my guess! I worked to that end as cautiously as possible, but all to no purpose; and finally I started abruptly toward the spot whence the sound had come, expecting to see the bird fly. But apparently there was no bird there, and I stood still, in a little perplexity. Then, all at once, the wren appeared, hopping about among the dead branches, within a few yards of my feet, and peering at the intruder with evident curiosity; and the next moment he was joined by a hermit thrush, equally inquisitive. Both were silent as dead men, but plainly had no doubt whatever that they were in their own domain, and that it belonged to the other party to move away. I presumed that the thrush, at least, had a nest not far off, but after a little search (the mosquitoes were still active) I concluded not to intrude further on his domestic privacy. I had heard the wren's famous song, and it had not been over-praised. But then came the inevitable second thought: had I really heard it? True, the music possessed the wren characteristics, and a winter wren was in the brush; but what proof had I that the bird and the song belonged together? No; I must see him in the act of singing. But this, I found, was more easily said than done. In Jefferson, in Gorham, in the Franconia Notch, in short, wherever I went, there was no difficulty about hearing the music, and little about seeing the wren; but it was provoking that eye and ear could never be brought to bear witness to the same bird. However, this difficulty was not insuperable, and after it was once overcome I was in the habit of witnessing the whole performance almost as often as I wished.

Of similar interest to me is a turn in an old Massachusetts road, over which, boy and man, I have traveled hundreds of times; one of those delightful back-roads, half road and half lane, where the grass grows between the horse-track and the wheel-track, while bushes usurp what ought to be the sidewalk. Here, one morning in the time when every day was disclosing two or three new species for my delight, I stopped to listen to some bird of quite unsuspected identity, who was calling and singing and scolding in the Indian brier thicket, making, in truth, a prodigious racket. I twisted and turned, and was not a little astonished when at last I detected the author of all this outcry. From a study of the manual I set him down as probably the white-eyed vireo,—a conjecture which further investigation confirmed. This vireo is the very prince of stump-speakers,—fluent, loud, and sarcastic,— and is well called the politician, though it is a disappointment to learn that the title was given him, not for his eloquence, but on account of his habit of putting pieces of newspaper into his nest. While I stood peering into the thicket, a man whom I knew came along the road, and caught me thus disreputably employed. Without doubt he thought me a lazy good-for-nothing; or possibly (being more charitable) he said to himself, "Poor fellow! he's losing his mind."

Take a gun on your shoulder, and go wandering about the woods all day long, and you will be looked upon with respect, no matter though you kill nothing bigger than a chipmunk; or stand by the hour at the end of a fishing-pole, catching nothing but mosquito-bites, and your neighbors will think no ill of you. But to be seen staring at a bird for five minutes together, or picking roadside weeds!—well, it is fortunate there are asylums for the crazy. Not unlikely the malady will grow upon him; and who knows how soon he may become dangerous? Something must be wrong about that to which we are unaccustomed. Blowing out the brains of rabbits and squirrels is an innocent and delightful pastime, as everybody knows; and the delectable excitement of pulling half-grown fishes out of the pond to perish miserably on the bank, that, too, is a recreation easily enough appreciated. But what shall be said of enjoying birds without killing them, or of taking pleasure in plants, which, so far as we know, cannot suffer even if we do kill them?

Of my many pleasant associations of birds with places, one of the pleasantest is connected with the red-headed woodpecker. This showy bird has for a good many years been very rare in Massachusetts; and therefore, when, during the freshness of my ornithological researches, I went to Washington for a month's visit, it was one of the things which I had especially in mind, to make his acquaintance. But I looked for him without success, till, at the end of a fortnight, I made a pilgrimage to Mount Vernon. Here, after visiting the grave, and going over the house, as every visitor does, I sauntered about the grounds, thinking of the great man who used to do the same so many years before, but all the while keeping my eyes open for the present feathered inhabitants of the sacred spot. Soon a bird dashed by me, and struck against the trunk of an adjacent tree, and glancing up quickly, I beheld my much- sought red-headed woodpecker. How appropriately patriotic he looked, at the home of Washington, wearing the national colors,—red, white, and blue! After this he became abundant about the capital, so that I saw him often, and took much pleasure in his frolicsome ways; and, some years later, he suddenly appeared in force in the vicinity of Boston, where he remained through the winter months. To my thought, none the less, he will always suggest Mount Vernon. Indeed, although he is certainly rather jovial, and even giddy, he is to me the bird of Washington much more truly than is the solemn, stupid-seeming eagle, who commonly bears that name.

To go away from home, even if the journey be no longer than from Massachusetts to the District of Columbia, is sure to prove an event of no small interest to a young naturalist; and this visit of mine to the national capital was no exception. On the afternoon of my arrival, walking up Seventh Street, I heard a series of loud, clear, monotonous whistles, which I had then no leisure to investigate, but the author of which I promised myself the satisfaction of meeting at another time. In fact, I think it was at least a fortnight before I learned that these whistles came from the tufted titmouse. I had been seeing him almost daily, but till then he had never chanced to use that particular note while under my eye.

There was a certain tract of country, woodland and pasture, over which I roamed a good many times, and which is still clearly mapped out in my memory. Here I found my first Carolina or mocking wren, who ran in at one side of a woodpile and came out at the other as I drew near, and who, a day or two afterwards, sang so loudly from an oak tree that I ransacked it with my eye in search of some large bird, and was confounded when finally I discovered who the musician really was. Here, every day, were to be heard the glorious song of the cardinal grosbeak, the insect-like effort of the blue-gray gnatcatcher, and the rigmarole of the yellow-breasted chat. On a wooded hillside, where grew a profusion of trailing arbutus, pink azalea, and bird-foot violets, the rowdyish, great-crested flycatchers were screaming in the tree-tops. In this same grove I twice saw the rare red-bellied woodpecker, who, on both occasions, after rapping smartly with his beak, turned his head and laid his ear against the trunk, evidently listening to see whether his alarm had set any grub a-stirring. Near by, in an undergrowth, I fell in with a few worm-eating warblers. They seemed of a peculiarly unsuspicious turn of mind, and certainly wore the quaintest of head-dresses. I must mention also a scarlet tanager, who, all afire as he was, one day alighted in a bush of flowering dogwood, which was completely covered with its large white blossoms. Probably he had no idea how well his perch became him.

Perhaps I ought to be ashamed to confess it, but, though I went several times into the galleries of our honorable Senate and House of Representatives, and heard speeches by some celebrated men, including at least half a dozen candidates for the presidency, yet, after all, the congressmen in feathers interested me most. I thought, indeed, that the chat might well enough have been elected to the lower house. His volubility and waggish manners would have made him quite at home in that assembly, while his orange-colored waistcoat would have given him an agreeable conspicuity. But, to be sure, he would have needed to learn the use of tobacco.

Well, all this was only a few years ago; but the men whose eloquence then drew the crowd to the capitol are, many of them, heard there no longer. Some are dead; some have retired to private life. But the birds never die. Every spring they come trooping back for their all-summer session. The turkey-buzzard still floats majestically over the city; the chat still practices his lofty tumbling in the suburban pastures, snarling and scolding at all comers; the flowing Potomac still yields "a blameless sport" to the fish-crow and the kingfisher; the orchard oriole continues to whistle in front of the Agricultural Department, and the crow blackbird to parade back and forth over the Smithsonian lawns. Presidents and senators may come and go, be praised and vilified, and then in turn forgotten; but the birds are subject to no such mutations. It is a foolish thought, but sometimes their happy carelessness seems the better part.

MINOR SONGSTERS.

The lesser lights, the dearer still
That they elude a vulgar eye.

— Browning.

Listen too,
How every pause is filled with under-notes.

— Shelley.

MINOR SONGSTERS.

Among those of us who are in the habit of attending to bird-songs, there can hardly be anybody, I think, who has not found himself specially and permanently attracted by the music of certain birds who have little or no general reputation. Our favoritism may perhaps be the result of early associations: we heard the singer first in some uncommonly romantic spot, or when we were in a mood of unusual sensibility; and, in greater or less degree, the charm of that hour is always renewed for us with the repetition of the song. Or if may be (who will assert the contrary?) that there is some occult relation between the bird's mind and our own. Or, once more, something may be due to the natural pleasure which amiable people take (and all lovers of birds may be supposed, a priori, to belong to that class) in paying peculiar honor to merit which the world at large, less discriminating than they, has thus far failed to recognize, and in which, therefore, as by "right of discovery," they have a sort of proprietary interest. This, at least, is evident: our preference is not determined altogether by the intrinsic worth of the song; the mind is active, not passive, and gives to the music something from itself,—"the consecration and the poet's dream."

Furthermore, it is to be said that a singer—and a bird no less than a man—may be wanting in that fullness and scope of voice and that large measure of technical skill which are absolutely essential to the great artist, properly so called, and yet, within his own limitations, may be competent to please even the most fastidious ear. It is with birds as with other poets: the smaller gift need not be the less genuine; and they whom the world calls greatest, and whom we ourselves most admire, may possibly not be the ones who touch us most intimately, or to whom we return oftenest and with most delight.

This may be well illustrated by a comparison of the chickadee with the brown thrush. The thrush, or, as he is sometimes profanely styled, the thrasher, is the most pretentious, perhaps I ought to say the greatest, of New England songsters, if we rule out the mocking-bird, who is so very rare with us as scarcely to come into the competition; and still, in my opinion, his singing seldom produces the effect of really fine music. With all his ability, which is nothing short of marvelous, his taste is so deplorably uncertain, and his passion so often becomes a downright frenzy, that the excited listener, hardly knowing what to think, laughs and shouts. Bravo! by turns. Something must be amiss, certainly, when the deepest feelings of the heart are poured forth in a manner to suggest the performance of a buffo. The chickadee, on the other hand, seldom gets mention as a singer. Probably he never looked upon himself as such. You will not find him posing at the top of a tree, challenging the world to listen and admire. But, as he hops from twig to twig in quest of insects' eggs and other dainties, his merry spirits are all the time bubbling over in little chirps and twitters, with now and then a Chickadee, dee, or a Hear, hear me, every least syllable of which is like "the very sound of happy thoughts." For my part, I rate such trifles with the best of all good music, and feel that we cannot be grateful enough to the brave tit, who furnishes us with them for the twelve months of every year.

So far as the chickadee is concerned, I see nothing whatever to wish different; but am glad to believe that, for my day and long after, he will remain the same unassuming, careless-hearted creature that he now is. If I may be allowed the paradox, it would be too bad for him to change, even for the better. But the bluebird, who like the titmouse is hardly to be accounted a musician, does seem to be somewhat blameworthy. Once in a while, it is true, he takes a perch and sings; but for the most part he is contented with a few simple notes, having no semblance of a tune. Possibly he holds that his pure contralto voice (I do not remember ever to have heard from him any note of a soprano, or even of a mezzo-soprano quality) ought by itself to be a sufficient distinction; but I think it likelier that his slight attempt at music is only one manifestation of the habitual reserve which, more than anything else perhaps, may be said to characterize him. How differently he and the robin impress us in this particular! Both take up their abode in our door-yards and orchards; the bluebird goes so far, indeed, as to accept our hospitality outright, building his nest in boxes put up for his accommodation, and making the roofs of our houses his favorite perching stations. But, while the robin is noisily and jauntily familiar, the bluebird maintains a dignified aloofness; coming and going about the premises, but keeping his thoughts to himself, and never becoming one of us save by the mere accident of local proximity. The robin, again, loves to travel in large flocks, when household duties are over for the season; but although the same has been reported of the bluebird, I have never myself seen such a thing, and am satisfied that, as a rule, this gentle spirit finds a family party of six or seven company enough. His reticence, as we cheerfully admit, is nothing to quarrel with; it is all well-bred, and not in the least unkindly; in fact, we like it, on the whole, rather better than the robin's pertness and garrulity; but, none the less, its natural consequence is that the bird has small concern for musical display. When he sings, it is not to gain applause, but to express his affection; and while, in one aspect of the case, there is nothing out of the way in this,—since his affection need not be the less deep and true because it is told in few words and with unadorned phrase,—yet, as I said to begin with, it is hard not to feel that the world is being defrauded, when for any reason, however amiable, the possessor of such a matchless voice has no ambition to make the most of it.

It is always a double pleasure to find a plodding, humdrum-seeming man with a poet's heart in his breast; and a little of the same delighted surprise is felt by every one, I imagine, when he learns for the first time that our little brown creeper is a singer. What life could possibly be more prosaic than his? Day after day, year in and out, he creeps up one tree-trunk after another, pausing only to peer right and left into the crevices of the bark, in search of microscopic tidbits. A most irksome sameness, surely! How the poor fellow must envy the swallows, who live on the wing, and, as it were, have their home in heaven! So it is easy for us to think; but I doubt whether the creeper himself is troubled with such suggestions. He seems, to say the least, as well contented as the most of us; and, what is more, I am inclined to doubt whether any except "free moral agents," like ourselves, are ever wicked enough to find fault with the orderings of Divine Providence. I fancy, too, that we may have exaggerated the monotony of the creeper's lot. It can scarcely be that even his days are without their occasional pleasurable excitements. After a good many trees which yield little or nothing for his pains, he must now and then light upon one which is like Canaan after the wilderness,—"a land flowing with milk and honey." Indeed, the longer I think of it the more confident I feel that every aged creeper must have had sundry experiences of this sort, which he is never weary of recounting for the edification of his nephews and nieces, who, of course, are far too young to have anything like the wide knowledge of the world which their venerable three-years-old uncle possesses. Certhia works all day for his daily bread; and yet even of him it is true that "the life is more than meat." He has his inward joys, his affectionate delights, which no outward infelicity can touch. A bird who thinks nothing of staying by his nest and his mate at the sacrifice of his life is not to be written down a dullard or a drudge, merely because his dress is plain and his occupation unromantic. He has a right to sing, for he has something within him to inspire the strain.

There are descriptions of the creeper's music which liken it to a wren's. I am sorry that I have myself heard it only on one occasion: then, however, so far was it from being wren-like that it might rather have been the work of one of the less proficient warblers,—a somewhat long opening note followed by a hurried series of shorter ones, the whole given in a sharp, thin voice, and having nothing to recommend it to notice, considered simply as music. All the while the bird kept on industriously with his journey up the tree; and it is not in the least unlikely that he may have another and better song, which he reserves for times of more leisure.[19]

Our American wood-warblers are all to be classed among the minor songsters; standing in this respect in strong contrast with the true Old World warblers, of whose musical capacity enough, perhaps, is said when

---

19. Since this was written I have heard the creeper sing a tune very different from the one described above. See p. 227.

it is mentioned that the nightingale is one of them. But, comparisons apart, our birds are by no means to be despised, and not a few of their songs have a good degree of merit. That of the well-known summer yellow-bird may be taken as fairly representative of the entire group, being neither one of the best nor one of the poorest. He, I have noticed, is given to singing late in the day. Three of the New England species have at the same time remarkably rough voices and black throats,—I mean the black-throated blue, the black-throated green, and the blue golden-wing,—and seeing that the first two are of the genus Dendrœca, while the last is a Helminthophaga, I have allowed myself to query (half in earnest) whether they may not, possibly, be more nearly related than the systematists have yet discovered. Several of the warbler songs are extremely odd. The blue yellow-back's, for example, is a brief, hoarse, upward run,—a kind of scale exercise; and if the practice of such things be really as beneficial as music teachers affirm, it would seem that this little beauty must in time become a vocalist of the first order. Nearly the same might be said of the prairie warbler; but his étude is a little longer and less hurried, besides being in a higher key. I do not call to mind any bird who sings a downward scale. Having before spoken of the tendency of warblers to learn two or even three set tunes, I was the more interested when, last summer, I added another to my list of the species which aspire to this kind of liberal education. It was on the side of Mount Clinton that I heard two Blackburnians, both in full sight and within a few rods of each other, who were singing two entirely distinct songs. One of these—it is the common one, I think—ended quaintly with three or four short notes, like zip, zip, zip; while the other was not unlike a fraction of the winter wren's melody. Those who are familiar with the latter bird will perhaps recognize the phrase referred to if I call it the willie, willie, winkie,—with a triple accent on the first syllable of the last word. Most of the songs of this family are rather slight, but the extremest case known to me is that of the black-poll (Dendrœca striata), whose zee, zee, zee is almost ridiculously faint. You may hear it continually in the higher spruce forests of the White Mountains; but you will look a good many times before you discover its author, and not improbably will begin by taking it for the call of the kinglet. The music of the bay-breasted warbler is similar to the black-poll's, but hardly so weak and formless. It seems reasonable to believe not only that these two species are descended from a common ancestry, but that the divergence is of a comparatively recent date: even now the young of the year can be distinguished only with great difficulty, although the birds in full feather are clearly enough marked.

Warblers' songs are often made up of two distinct portions: one given deliberately, the other hurriedly and with a concluding flourish. Indeed, the same may be said of bird-songs generally,—those of the song sparrow, the bay-winged bunting, and the wood thrush being familiar examples. Yet there are many singers who attempt no climax of this sort, but make their music to consist of two, or three, or more parts, all alike. The Maryland yellow-throat, for instance, cries out over and over, "What a pity, what a pity, what a pity!" So, at least, he seems to say; though, I confess, it is more than likely I mistake the words, since the fellow never appears to be feeling badly, but, on the contrary, delivers his message with an air of cordial satisfaction. The song of the pine-creeping warbler is after still another fashion,—one simple short trill. It is musical and sweet; the more so for coming almost always out of a pine-tree.

The vireos, or greenlets, are akin to the warblers in appearance and habits, and like them are peculiar to the western continent. We have no birds that are more unsparing of their music (prodigality is one of the American virtues, we are told): they sing from morning till night, and—some of them, at least—continue thus till the very end of the season. It is worth mentioning, however, that the red-eye makes a short day; becoming silent just at the time when the generality of birds grow most noisy. Probably the same is true of the rest of the family, but on that point I am not prepared to speak with positiveness. Of the five New England species (I omit the brotherly-love greenlet, never having been fortunate enough to know him) the white-eye is decidedly the most ambitious, the warbling and the solitary are the most pleasing, while the red-eye and the yellow-throat are very much alike, and both of them rather too monotonous and persistent. It is hard, sometimes, not to get out of patience with the red-eye's ceaseless and noisy iteration of his trite theme; especially if you are doing your utmost to catch the notes of some rarer and more refined songster. In my note-book I find an entry describing my vain attempts to enjoy the music of a rose-breasted grosbeak,—who at that time had never been a common bird with me,—while "a pesky Wagnerian red-eye kept up an incessant racket."

The warbling vireo is admirably named; there is no one of our birds that can more properly be said to warble. He keeps further from the ground than the others, and shows a strong preference for the elms of village streets, out of which his delicious music drops upon the ears of all passers underneath. How many of them hear it and thank the singer is unhappily another question.

The solitary vireo may once in a while be heard in a roadside tree, chanting as familiarly as any red-eye; but he is much less abundant than the latter, and, as a rule, more retiring. His ordinary song is like the red-eye's and the yellow-throat's, except that it is pitched somewhat higher and has a peculiar inflection or cadence, which on sufficient acquaintance becomes quite unmistakable. This, however, is only the smallest part of his musical gift. One morning in May, while strolling through a piece of thick woods, I came upon a bird of this species, who, all alone like myself, was hopping from one low branch to another, and every now and then breaking out into a kind of soliloquizing song,—a musical chatter, shifting suddenly to an in tricate, low-voiced warble. Later in the same day I found another in a chestnut grove. This last was in a state of quite unwonted fervor, and sang almost continuously; now in the usual disconnected vireo manner, and now with a chatter and warble like what I had heard in the morning, but louder and longer. His best efforts ended abruptly with the ordinary vireo call, and the instantaneous change of voice gave to the whole a very strange effect. The chatter and warble appeared to be related to each other precisely as are those of the ruby-crowned kinglet; while the warble had a certain tender, affectionate, some would say plaintive quality, which at once put me in mind of the goldfinch.

I have seldom been more charmed with the song of any bird than I was on the 7th of last October with that of this same Vireo solitarius. The morning was bright and warm, but the birds had nearly all taken their departure, and the few that remained were silent. Suddenly the stillness was broken by a vireo note, and I said to myself with surprise, A red-eye? Listening again, however, I detected the solitary's inflection; and after a few moments the bird, in the most obliging manner, came directly towards me, and began to warble in the fashion already described. He sang and sang,—as if his song could have no ending,—

and mean while was flitting from tree to tree, intent upon his breakfast. As far as I could discover, he was without company; and his music, too, seemed to be nothing more than an unpremeditated, half-unconscious talking to himself. Wonderfully sweet it was, and full of the happiest content. "I listened till I had my fill," and returned the favor, as best I could, by hoping that the little wayfarer's lightsome mood would not fail him, all the way to Guatemala and back again.

Exactly a month before this, and not far from the same spot, I had stood for some minutes to enjoy the "recital" of the solitary's saucy cousin, the white-eye. Even at that time, although the woods were swarming with birds,—many of them travelers from the North,—this white-eye was nearly the only one still in song. He, however, was fairly brimming over with music; changing his tune again and again, and introducing (for the first time in Weymouth, as concert programmes say) a notably fine shake. Like the solitary, he was all the while busily feeding (birds in general, and vireos in particular, hold with Mrs. Browning that we may "prove our work the better for the sweetness of our song"), and one while was exploring a poison-dogwood bush, plainly without the slightest fear of any ill-result. It occurred to me that possibly it is our fault, and not that of Rhus venenata, when we suffer from the touch of that graceful shrub.

The white-eyed greenlet is a vocalist of such extraordinary versatility and power that one feels almost guilty in speaking of him under the title which stands at the head of this paper. How he would scold, out-carlyling Carlyle, if he knew what were going on! Nevertheless I cannot rank him with the great singers, exceptionally clever and original as, beyond all dispute, he is; and for that matter, I look upon the solitary as very much his superior, in spite of—or, shall I say, because of?—the latter's greater simplicity and reserve.

But if we hesitate thus about these two inconspicuous vireos, whom half of those who do them the honor to read what is here said about them will have never seen, how are we to deal with the scarlet tanager? Our handsomest bird, and with musical aspirations as well, shall we put him into the second class? It must be so, I fear: yet such justice is a trial to the flesh; for what critic could ever quite leave out of account the beauty of a prima donna in passing judgment on her work? Does not her angelic face sing to his eye, as Emerson says?

Formerly I gave the tanager credit for only one song,—the one which suggests a robin laboring under an attack of hoarseness; but I have discovered that he himself regards his chip-cherr as of equal value. At least, I have found him perched at the tip of a tall pine, and repeating this inconsiderable and not very melodious trochee with all earnestness and perseverance. Sometimes he rehearses it thus at nightfall; but even so I cannot call it highly artistic. I am glad to believe, however, that he does not care in the least for my opinion. Why should he? He is too true a gallant to mind what anybody else thinks, so long as one is pleased; and she, no doubt, tells him every day that he is the best singer in the grove. Beside his divine chip-cherr the rhapsody of the wood thrush is a mere nothing, if she is to be the judge. Strange, indeed, that so shabbily dressed a creature as this thrush should have the presumption to attempt to sing at all! "But then," she charitably adds, "perhaps he is not to blame; such things come by nature; and there are some birds, you know, who cannot tell the difference between noise and music."

We trust that the tanager will improve as time goes on; but in any case we are largely in his debt. How we should miss him if he were gone, or even were become as rare as the summer red-bird and the cardinal are in our latitude! As it is, he lights up our Northern woods with a truly tropical splendor, the like of which no other of our birds can furnish. Let us hold him in hearty esteem, and pray that he may never be exterminated; no, not even to beautify the head-gear of our ladies, who, if they only knew it, are already sufficiently bewitching.

What shall we say now about the lesser lights of that most musical family, the finches? Of course the cardinal and rose-breasted grosbeaks are not to be included in any such category. Nor will I put there the goldfinch, the linnet, the fox-colored sparrow, and the song sparrow. These, if no more, shall stand among the immortals; so far, at any rate, as my suffrage counts. But who ever dreamed of calling the chipping sparrow a fine singer? And yet, who that knows it does not love his earnest, long-drawn trill, dry and tuneless as it is? I can speak for one, at all events; and he always has an ear open for it by the middle of April. It is the voice of a friend,—a friend so true and gentle and confiding that we do not care to ask whether his voice be smooth and his speech eloquent.

The chipper's congener, the field sparrow, is less neighborly than he, but a much better musician. His song is simplicity itself; yet, even at its lowest estate, it never fails of being truly melodious, while by one means and another its wise little author contrives to impart to it a very considerable variety, albeit within pretty narrow limits. Last spring the field sparrows were singing constantly from the middle of April till about the 10th of May, when they became entirely dumb. Then, after a week in which I heard not a note, they again grew musical. I pondered not a little over their silence, but concluded that they were just then very much occupied with preparations for housekeeping.

The bird who is called indiscriminately the grass finch, the bay-winged bunting, the bay-winged sparrow, the vesper sparrow, and I know not what else (the ornithologists have nicknamed him Poœcetes gramineus), is a singer of good parts, but is especially to be commended for his refinement. In form his music is strikingly like the song sparrow's; but the voice is not so loud and ringing, and the two or three opening notes are less sharply emphasized. In general the difference between the two songs may perhaps be well expressed by saying that the one is more declamatory, the other more cantabile; a difference exactly such as we might have expected, considering the nervous, impetuous disposition of the song sparrow and the placidity of the bay-wing.

As one of his titles indicates, the bay-wing is famous for singing in the evening, when, of course, his efforts are doubly acceptable; and I can readily believe that Mr. Minot is correct in his "impression" that he has once or twice heard the song in the night. For while spending a few days at a New Hampshire hotel, which was surrounded with fine lawns such as the grass finch delights in, I happened to be awake in the morning, long before sunrise,—when, in fact, it seemed like the dead of night,—and one or two of these sparrows were piping freely. The sweet and gentle strain had the whole mountain valley to itself. How beautiful it was, set in such a broad "margin of silence," I must leave to be imagined. I noticed, moreover, that the birds sang almost incessantly the whole day through. Much of the time there were two singing antiphonally. Manifestly, the lines had fallen to them in pleasant places: at home for the summer in those luxuriant Sugar-Hill fields, in continual sight of yonder magnificent mountain panorama, with Lafayette himself looming grandly in the foreground; while they, innocent souls, had never so much as heard of hotel-keepers and their bills. "Happy commoners," indeed! Their "songs in the night" seemed nowise surprising. I fancied that I could be happy myself in such a case.

Our familiar and ever-welcome snow-bird, known in some quarters as the black chipping-bird, and often called the black snow-bird, has a long trill, not altogether unlike the common chipper's, but in a much higher key. It is a modest lay, yet doubtless full of meaning; for the singer takes to the very tip of a tree, and throws his head back in the most approved style. He does his best, at any rate, and so far ranks with the angels; while, if my testimony can be of any service to him, I am glad to say ('t is too bad the praise is so equivocal) that I have heard many human singers who gave me less pleasure; and further, that he took an indispensable though subordinate part in what was one of the most memorable concerts at which I was ever happy enough to be a listener. This was given some years ago in an old apple-orchard by a flock of fox-colored sparrows, who, perhaps for that occasion only, had the "valuable assistance" of a large choir of snow-birds. The latter were twittering in every tree, while to this goodly accompaniment the sparrows were singing their loud, clear, thrush-like song. The combination was felicitous in the extreme. I would go a long way to hear the like again.

If distinction cannot be attained by one means, who knows but that it may be by another? It is denied us to be great? Very well, we can at least try the effect of a little originality. Something like this seems to be the philosophy of the indigo-bird; and he carries it out both in dress and in song. As we have said already, it is usual for birds to reserve the loudest and most taking parts of their music for the close, though it may be doubted whether they have any intelligent purpose in so doing. Indeed, the apprehension of a great general truth such as lies at the basis of this well-nigh universal habit,—the truth, namely, that everything depends upon the impression finally left on the hearer's mind; that to end with some grand burst, or with some surprisingly lofty note, is the only, or to speak cautiously, the principal, requisite to a really great musical performance,—the intelligent grasp of such a truth as this, I say, seems to me to lie beyond the measure of a bird's capacity in the present stage of his development. Be this as it may, however, it is noteworthy that the indigo-bird exactly reverses the common plan. He begins at his loudest and sprightliest, and then runs off into a diminuendo, which fades into silence almost imperceptibly. The strain will never be renowned for its beauty; but it is unique, and, further, is continued well into August. Moreover,—and this adds grace to the most ordinary song,—it is often let fall while the bird is on the wing.

This eccentric genius has taken possession of a certain hillside pasture, which, in another way, belongs to me also. Year after year he comes back and settles down upon it about the middle of May; and I have often been amused to see his mate—who is not permitted to wear a single blue feather—drop out of her nest in a barberry bush and go fluttering off, both wings dragging helplessly through the grass. I should pity her profoundly but that I am in no doubt her injuries will rapidly heal when once I am out of sight. Besides, I like to imagine her beatitude, as, five minutes afterward, she sits again upon the nest, with her heart's treasures all safe underneath her. Many a time was a boy of my acquaintance comforted in some ache or pain with the words, "Never mind! 't will feel better when it gets well;" and so, sure enough, it always did. But what a wicked world this is, where nature teaches even a bird to play the deceiver!

On the same hillside is always to be found the chewink,—a creature whose dress and song are so unlike those of the rest of his tribe that the irreverent amateur is tempted to believe that, for once, the men of science have made a mistake. What has any finch to do with a call like cherawink, or with such a three-colored harlequin suit? But it is unsafe to judge according to the outward appearance, in ornithology as in other matters; and I have heard that it is only those who are foolish as well as ignorant who indulge in off-hand criticisms of wiser men's conclusions. So let us call the towhee a finch, and say no more about it.

But whatever his lineage, it is plain that the chewink is not a bird to be governed very strictly by the traditions of the fathers. His usual song is characteristic and pretty, yet he is so far from being satisfied with it that he varies it continually and in many ways, some of them sadly puzzling to the student who is set upon telling all the birds by their voices. I remember well enough the morning I was inveigled through the wet grass of two pastures—and that just as I was shod for the city—by a wonderfully foreign note, which filled me with lively anticipations of a new bird, but which turned out to be the work of a most innocent-looking towhee. It was perhaps this same bird, or his brother, whom I one day heard throwing in between his customary cherawinks a profusion of staccato notes of widely varying pitch, together with little volleys of tinkling sounds such as his every-day song concludes with. This medley was not laughable, like the chat's, which it suggested, but it had the same abrupt, fragmentary, and promiscuous character. All in all, it was what I never should have expected from this paragon of self-possession.

For self-control, as I have elsewhere said, is Pipilo's strong point. One afternoon last summer a young friend and I found ourselves, as we suspected, near a chewink's nest, and at once set out to see which of us should have the honor of the discovery. We searched diligently, but without avail, while the father-bird sat quietly in a tree, calling with all sweetness and with never a trace of anger or trepidation, cherawink, cherawink. Finally we gave over the hunt, and I began to console my companion and myself for our disappointment by shaking in the face of the bird a small tree which very conveniently leaned toward the one in which he was perched. By rather vigorous efforts I could make this pass back and forth within a few inches of his bill; but he utterly disdained to notice it, and kept on calling as before. While we were laughing at his impudence (his impudence!) the mother suddenly appeared, with an insect in her beak, and joined her voice to her husband's. I was just declaring how cruel as well as useless it was for us to stay, when she ungratefully gave a ludicrous turn to what was intended for a very sage and considerate remark, by dropping almost at my feet, stepping upon the edge of her nest, and offering the morsel to one of her young. We watched the little tableau admiringly (I had never seen a prettier show of nonchalance), and thanked our stars that we had been saved from an involuntary slaughter of the innocents while trampling all about the spot. The nest, which we had tried so hard to find, was in plain sight, concealed only by the perfect agreement of its color with that of the dead pine-branches in the midst of which it was placed. The shrewd birds had somehow learned—by experience, perhaps, like ourselves—that those who would escape disagreeable and perilous conspicuity must conform as closely as possible to the world around them.

According to my observation, the towhee is not much given to singing after July; but he keeps up his call, which is little less musical than his song, till his departure in late September. At that time of the year the birds collect together in their favorite haunts; and I remember my dog's running into the edge of a roadside pasture among some cedar-trees, when there broke out such a chorus of cherawinks that I was instantly reminded of a swamp full of frogs in April.

After the tanager the Baltimore oriole (named for Lord Baltimore, whose colors he wears) is probably the most gorgeous, as he is certainly one of the best known, of New England birds. He has discovered that men, bad as they are, are less to be dreaded than hawks and weasels, and so, after making sure that his wife is not subject to sea-sickness, he swings his nest boldly from a swaying shade-tree branch, in full view of whoever may choose to look at it. Some morning in May—not far from the 10th—you will wake to hear him fifing in the elm before your window. He has come in the night, and is already making himself at home. Once I saw a pair who on the very first morning had begun to get together materials for a nest. His whistle is one of the clearest and loudest, but he makes little pretensions to music. I have been pleased and interested, however, to see how tuneful he becomes in August, after most other birds have ceased to sing, and after a long interval of silence on his own part. Early and late he pipes and chatters, as if he imagined that the spring were really coming back again forthwith. What the explanation of this lyrical revival may be I have never been able to gather; but the fact itself is very noticeable, so that it would not be amiss to call the "golden robin" the bird of August.

The oriole's dusky relatives have the organs of song well developed; and although most of the species have altogether lost the art of music, there are none of them, even now, that do not betray more or less of the musical impulse. The red-winged blackbird, indeed, has some really praiseworthy notes; and to me—for personal reasons quite aside from any question about its lyrical value—his rough cucurree is one of the very pleasantest of sounds. For that matter, however, there is no one of our birds—be he, in technical language, "oscine" or "non-oscine"—whose voice is not, in its own way, agreeable. Except a few uncommonly superstitious people, who does not enjoy the whip-poor-will's trisyllabic exhortation, and the yak of the night-hawk? Bob White's weather predictions, also, have a wild charm all their own, albeit his persistent No more wet is often sadly out of accord with the farmer's hopes. We have no more untuneful bird, surely, than the cow bunting; yet even the serenades of this shameless polygamist have one merit,—they are at least amusing. With what infinite labor he brings forth his forlorn, broken-winded whistle, while his tail twitches convulsively, as if tail and larynx were worked by the same spring!

The judging, comparing spirit, the conscientious dread of being ignorantly happy when a broader culture would enable us to be intelligently miserable,—this has its place, unquestionably, in concert halls; but if we are to make the best use of out-door minstrelsy, we must learn to take things as we find them, throwing criticism to the winds. Having said which, I am bound to go further still, and to acknowledge that on looking back over the first part of this paper I feel more than half ashamed of the strictures therein passed upon the bluebird and the brown thrush. When I heard the former's salutation from a Boston Common elm on the morning, of the 22d of February last, I said to myself that no music, not even the nightingale's, could ever be sweeter. Let him keep on, by all means, in his own artless way, paying no heed to what I have foolishly written about his shortcomings. As for the thrasher's smile-provoking gutturals, I recall that even in the symphonies of the greatest of masters there are here and there quaint bassoon phrases, which have, and doubtless were intended to have, a somewhat whimsical effect; and remembering this, I am ready to own that I was less wise than I thought myself when I found so much fault with the thrush's performance. I have sins enough to answer for: may this never be added to them, that I set up my taste against that of Beethoven and Harporhynchus rufus.

WINTER BIRDS ABOUT BOSTON.

Not much to find, not much to see;
But the air was fresh, the path was free.

— W. Allingham.

WINTER BIRDS ABOUT BOSTON.

A weed has been defined as a plant the use of which is not yet discovered. If the definition be correct there are few weeds. For the researches of others beside human investigators must be taken into the account. What we complacently call the world below us is full of intelligence. Every animal has a lore of its own; not one of them but is—what the human scholar is more and more coming to be—a specialist. In these days the most eminent botanists are not ashamed to compare notes with the insects, since it turns out that these bits of animate wisdom long ago anticipated some of the latest improvements of our modern systematists.[20] We may see the red squirrel eating, with real epicurean zest, mushrooms, the white and tender flesh of which we have ourselves looked at longingly, but have never dared to taste. How amused he would be (I fear he would even be rude enough to snicker) were you to caution him against poison! As if Sciurus Hudsonius didn't know what he were about! Why should men be so provincial as to pronounce anything worthless merely because they can do nothing with it? The clover is not without value, although the robin and the oriole may agree to think so. We know better; and so do the rabbits and the humblebees. The wise respect their own quality wherever they see it,

20. See a letter by Dr. Fritz Müller, "Butterflies as Botanists:" Nature, vol. xxx. p. 240. Of similar import is the case, cited by Dr. Asa Gray (in the American Journal of Science, November, 1884, p. 325), of two species of plantain found in this country, which students have only of late discriminated, although it turns out that the cows have all along known them apart, eating one and declining the other,—the bovine taste being more exact, it would seem, or at any rate more prompt, than the botanist's lens.

and are thankful for a good hint from no matter what quarter. Here is a worthy neighbor of mine whom I hear every summer complaining of the chicory plants which disfigure the roadside in front of her windows. She wishes they were exterminated, every one of them. And they are homely, there is no denying it, for all the beauty of their individual sky-blue flowers. No wonder a neat housewife finds them an eyesore. But I never pass the spot in August (I do not pass it at all after that) without seeing that hers is only one side of the story. My approach is sure to startle a few goldfinches (and they too are most estimable neighbors), to whom these scraggy herbs are quite as useful as my excellent lady's apple-trees and pear-trees are to her. I watch them as they circle about in musical undulations, and then drop down again to finish their repast; and I perceive that, in spite of its unsightliness, the chicory is not a weed,—its use has been discovered.

In truth, the lover of birds soon ceases to feel the uncomeliness of plants of this sort; he even begins to have a peculiar and kindly interest in them. A piece of "waste ground," as it is called, an untidy garden, a wayside thicket of golden-rods and asters, pig-weed and evening primrose,—these come to be almost as attractive a sight to him as a thrifty field of wheat is to an agriculturalist. Taking his cue from the finches, he separates plants into two grand divisions,—those that shed their seeds in the fall, and those that hold them through the winter. The latter, especially if they are of a height to overtop a heavy snow-fall, are friends in need to his clients; and he is certain to have marked a few places within the range of his every-day walks where, thanks to somebody's shiftlessness, perhaps, they have been allowed to flourish.

It is not many years since there were several such winter gardens of the birds in Commonwealth Avenue,—vacant house-lots overgrown with tall weeds. Hither cause flocks of goldfinches, red-poll linnets, and snow buntings; and thither I went to watch them. It happened, I remember, that the last two species, which are not to be met with in this region every season, were unusually abundant during the first or second year of my ornithological enthusiasm. Great was the delight with which I added them to the small but rapidly increasing list of my feathered acquaintances.

The red-polls and the goldfinches often travel together, or at least are often to be found feeding in company; and as they resemble each other a good deal in size, general appearance, and ways, the casual observer is very likely not to discriminate between them. Only the summer before the time of which I speak I had spent a vacation at Mount Wachusett; and a resident of Princeton, noticing my attention to the birds (a taste so peculiar is not easily concealed), had one day sought an interview with me to inquire whether the "yellow-bird" did not remain in Massachusetts through the winter. I explained that we had two birds which commonly went by that name and asked whether he meant the one with a black forehead and black wings and tail. Yes, he said, that was the one. I assured him, of course, that this bird, the goldfinch, did stay with us all the year round, and that whoever had informed him to the contrary must have understood him to be speaking about the golden warbler. He expressed his gratification, but declared that he had really entertained no doubt of the fact himself; he had often seen the birds on the mountain when he had been cutting wood there in midwinter. At such times, he added, they were very tame, and would come about his feet to pick up crumbs while he was eating his dinner. Then he went on to tell me that at that season of the year their plumage took on more or less of a reddish tinge: he had seen in the same flock some with no trace of red, others that were slightly touched with it, and others still of a really bright color. At this I had nothing to say, save that his red birds, whatever else they were, could not have been goldfinches. But next winter, when I saw the "yellow-birds" and the red-poll linnets feeding together in Commonwealth Avenue, I thought at once of my Wachusett friend. Here was the very scene he had so faithfully described,—some of the flock with no red at all, some with red crowns, and a few with bright carmine crowns and breasts. They remained all winter, and no doubt thought the farmers of Boston a very good and wise set, to cultivate the evening primrose so extensively. This plant, like the succory, is of an ungraceful aspect; yet it has sweet and beautiful blossoms, and as an herb bearing seed is in the front rank. I doubt whether we have any that surpass it, the birds being judges.

Many stories are told of the red-polls' fearlessness and ready reconciliation to captivity, as well as of their constancy to each other. I have myself stood still in the midst of a flock, until they were feeding round my feet so closely that it looked easy enough to catch one or two of them with a butterfly net. Strange that creatures so gentle and seemingly so delicately organized should choose to live in the regions about the North Pole! Why should they prefer Labrador and Greenland, Iceland and Spitzbergen, to more southern countries? Why? Well, possibly for no worse a reason than this, that these are the lands of their fathers. Other birds, it may be, have grown discouraged, and one after another ceased to come back to their native shores as the rigors of the climate have increased; but these little patriots are still faithful. Spitzbergen is home, and every spring they make the long and dangerous passage to it. All praise to them!

If any be ready to call this an over-refinement, deeming it incredible that beings so small and lowly should come so near to human sentiment and virtue, let such not be too hasty with their dissent. Surely they may in reason wait till they can point to at least one country where the men are as universally faithful to their wives and children as the birds are to theirs.

The red-poll linnets, as I have said, are irregular visitors in this region; several years may pass, and not one be seen; but the goldfinch we have with us always. Easily recognized as he is, there are many well-educated New-Englanders, I fear, who do not know him, even by sight; yet when that distinguished ornithologist, the Duke of Argyll, comes to publish his impressions of this country, he avers that he has been hardly more interested in the "glories of Niagara" than in this same little yellow-bird, which he saw for the first time while looking from his hotel window at the great cataract. "A golden finch, indeed!" he exclaims. Such a tribute as this from the pen of a British nobleman ought to give Astragalinus tristis immediate entrance into the very best of American society.

It is common to say that the goldfinches wander about the country during the winter. Undoubtedly this is true in a measure; but I have seen things which lead me to suspect that the statement is sometimes made too sweeping. Last winter, for example, a flock took up their quarters in a certain neglected piece of ground on the side of Beacon Street, close upon the boundary between Boston and Brookline, and remained there nearly or quite the whole season. Week after week I saw them in the same place, accompanied always by half a dozen tree sparrows. They had found a spot to their mind, with plenty of succory and evening primrose, and were wise enough not to forsake it for any uncertainty.

The goldfinch loses his bright feathers and canary-like song as the cold season approaches, but not even a New England winter can rob him of his sweet call and his cheerful spirits; and for one, I think him never more winsome than when he bangs in graceful attitudes above a snow-bank, on a bleak January morning.

Glad as we are of the society of the goldfinches and the red-polls at this time of the year, we cannot easily rid ourselves of a degree of solicitude for their comfort; especially if we chance to come upon them after sunset on some bitterly cold day, and mark with what a nervous haste they snatch here and there a seed, making the utmost of the few remaining minutes of twilight. They will go to bed hungry and cold, we think, and were surely better off in a milder clime. But, if I am to judge from my own experience, the snow buntings awaken no such emotions. Arctic explorers by instinct, they come to us only with real arctic weather, and almost seem to be themselves a part of the snow-storm with which they arrive. No matter what they are doing: running along the street before an approaching sleigh; standing on a wayside fence; jumping up from the ground to snatch the stem of a weed, and then setting at work hurriedly to gather the seeds they have shaken down; or, best of all, skimming over the snow in close order, their white breasts catching the sun as they veer this way or that,—whatever they may be doing, they are the most picturesque of all our cold-weather birds. In point of suspiciousness their behavior is very different at different times, as, for that matter, is true of birds generally. Seeing the flock alight in a low roadside lot, you steal silently to the edge of the sidewalk to look over upon them. There they are, sure enough, walking and running about, only a few rods distant. What lovely creatures, and how prettily they walk! But just as you are wishing, perhaps, that they were a little nearer, they begin to fly from right under your feet. You search the ground eagerly, right and left, but not a bird can you discover; and still they continue to start up, now here, now there, till you are ready to question whether, indeed, "eyes were made for seeing." The "snow-flakes" wear protective colors, and, like most other animals, are of opinion that, for such as lack the receipt of fern-seed, there is often nothing safer than to sit still. The worse the weather, the less timorous they are, for with them, as with wiser heads, one thought drives out another; and it is nothing uncommon, when times are hard, to see them stay quietly upon the fence while a sleigh goes past, or suffer a foot passenger to come again and again within a few yards.

It gives a lively touch to the imagination to overtake these beautiful strangers in the middle of Beacon Street; particularly if one has lately been reading about them in some narrative of Siberian travel. Coming from so far, associating in flocks, with costumes so becoming and yet so unusual, they might be expected to attract universal notice, and possibly to get into the newspapers. But there is a fashion even about seeing; and of a thousand persons who may take a Sunday promenade over the Mill-dam, while these tourists from the North Pole are there, it is doubtful whether a dozen are aware of their presence. Birds feeding in the street? Yes, yes; English sparrows, of course; we haven't any other birds in Boston nowadays, you know.

With the pine grosbeaks the case is different. When a man sees a company of rather large birds about the evergreens in his door-yard, most of them of a neutral ashy-gray tint, but one or two in suits of rose-color, he is pretty certain to feel at least a momentary curiosity about them. Their slight advantage in size counts for something; for, without controversy, the bigger the bird the more worthy he is of notice. And then the bright color! The very best men are as yet but imperfectly civilized, and there must be comparatively few, even of Bostonians, in whom there is not some lingering susceptibility to the fascination of red feathers. Add to these things the fact that the grosbeaks are extremely confiding, and much more likely than the buntings to be seen from the windows of the house, and you have, perhaps, a sufficient explanation of the more general interest they excite. Like the snow buntings and the red-polls, they roam over the higher latitudes of Europe, Asia, and America, and make only irregular visits to our corner of the world.[21]

I cannot boast of any intimate acquaintance with them. I have never caught them in a net, or knocked them over with a club, as other per sons have done, although I have seen them when their tameness promised success to any such loving experiment. Indeed, it was several years before my lookout for them was rewarded. Then, one day, I saw a flock of about ten fly across Beacon Street,—on the edge of Brookline,—and

21. Unlike the snow bunting and the red-poll, however, the pine grosbeak is believed to breed sparingly in Northern New England.

alight in an apple-tree; at which I forthwith clambered over the picket-fence after them, heedless alike of the deep snow and the surprise of any steady-going citizen who might chance to witness my high-handed proceeding. Some of the birds were feeding upon the rotten apples; picking them off the tree, and taking them to one of the large main branches or to the ground, and there tearing them to pieces,—for the sake of the seeds, I suppose. The rest sat still, doing nothing. I was most impressed with the exceeding mildness and placidity of their demeanor; as if they had time enough, plenty to eat, and nothing to fear. Their only notes were in quality much like the goldfinch's, and hardly louder, but without his characteristic inflection. I left the whole company seated idly in a maple-tree, where, to all appearance, they proposed to observe the remainder of the day as a Sabbath.

Last winter the grosbeaks were uncommonly abundant. I found a number of them within a few rods of the place just mentioned; this time in evergreen trees, and so near the road that I had no call to commit trespass. Evergreens are their usual resort,—so, at least, I gather from books,—but I have seen them picking up provender from a bare-looking last year's garden. Natives of the inhospitable North, they have learned by long experience how to adapt themselves to circumstances. If one resource fails, there is always another to be tried. Let us hope that they even know how to show fight upon, occasion.

The purple finch—a small copy of the pine grosbeak, as the indigo bird is of the blue grosbeak—is a summer rather than a winter bird with us; yet he sometimes passes the cold season in Eastern Massachusetts, and even in Northern New Hampshire. I have never heard him sing more gloriously than once when the ground was deep under the snow; a wonderfully sweet and protracted warble, poured out while the singer circled about in the air with a kind of half-hovering flight.

As I was walking briskly along a West End street, one cold morning in March, I heard a bird's note close at hand, and, looking down, discovered a pair of these finches in a front yard. The male, in bright plumage, was flitting about his mate, calling anxiously, while she, poor thing, sat motionless upon the snow, too sick or too badly exhausted to fly. I stroked her feathers gently while she perched on my finger, and then resumed my walk; first putting her into a little more sheltered position on the sill of a cellar window, and promising to call on my way back, when, if she were no better, I would take her home with me, and give her a warm room and good nursing. When I returned, however, she was nowhere to be found. Her mate, I regret to say, both on his own account and for the sake of the story, had taken wing and disappeared the moment I entered the yard. Possibly he came back and encouraged her to fly off with him; or perhaps some cat made a Sunday breakfast of her. The truth will never be known; our vigilant city police take no cognizance of tragedies so humble.

For several years a few song sparrows—a pair or two, at least—have wintered in a piece of ground just beyond the junction of Beacon street and Brookline Avenue. I have grown accustomed to listen for their tseep as I go by the spot, and occasionally I catch sight of one of them perched upon a weed, or diving under the plank sidewalk. It would be a pleasure to know the history of the colony: how it started; whether the birds are the same year after year, as I suppose to be the case; and why this particular site was selected. The lot is small, with no woods or bushy thicket near, while it has buildings in one corner, and is bounded on its three sides by the streets and the railway; but it is full of a rank growth of weeds, especially a sturdy species of aster and the evergreen golden-rod, and I suspect that the plank walk, which on one side is raised some distance from the ground, is found serviceable for shelter in severe weather, as it is certainly made to take the place of shrubbery for purposes of concealment.

Fortunately, birds, even those of the same species, are not all exactly alike in their tastes and manner of life. So, while by far the greater part of our song sparrows leave us in the fall, there are always some who prefer to stay. They have strong local attachments, perhaps; or they dread the fatigue and peril of the journey; or they were once incapacitated for flight when their companions went away, and, having found a Northern winter not so unendurable as they had expected, have since done from choice what at first they did of necessity. Whatever their reasons,—and we cannot be presumed to have guessed half of them,—at all events a goodly number of song sparrows do winter in Massachusetts, where they open the musical season before the first of the migrants make their appearance. I doubt, however, whether many of them choose camping grounds so exposed and public as this in the rear of the "Half-way House."

Our only cold-weather thrushes are the robins. They may be found any time in favorable situations; and even in so bleak a place as Boston Common I have seen them in every month of the year except February. This exception, moreover, is more apparent than real,—at the most a matter of but twenty-four hours, since I once saw four birds in a tree near the Frog Pond on the last day of January. The house sparrows were as much surprised as I was at the sight, and, with characteristic urbanity, gathered from far and near to sit in the same tree with the visitors, and stare at them.

We cannot help being grateful to the robins and the song sparrows, who give us their society at so great a cost; but their presence can scarcely be thought to enliven the season. At its best their bearing is only that of patient submission to the inevitable. They remind us of the summer gone and the summer coming, rather than brighten the winter that is now upon us; like friends who commiserate us in some affliction, but are not able to comfort us. How different the chickadee! In the worst weather his greeting is never of condolence, but of good cheer. He has no theory upon the subject, probably; he is no Shepherd of Salisbury Plain; but he knows better than to waste the exhilarating air of this wild and frosty day in reminiscences of summer time. It is a pretty-sounding couplet,—

"Thou hast no morrow in thy song,

No winter in thy year,"—

but rather incongruous, he would think. Chickadee, dee, he calls,—chickadee, dee; and though the words have no exact equivalent in English, their meaning is felt by all such as are worthy to hear them.

Are the smallest birds really the most courageous, or does an unconscious sympathy on our part inevitably give them odds in the comparison? Probably the latter supposition comes nearest the truth. When a sparrow chases a butcher-bird we cheer the sparrow, and then when a humming-bird puts to flight a sparrow, we cheer the humming-bird; we side with the kingbird against the crow, and with the vireo, against the kingbird. It is a noble trait of human nature—though we are somewhat too ready to boast of it—that we like, as we say, to see the little fellow at the top. These remarks are made, not with any reference to the chickadee,—I admit no possibility of exaggeration in his case,—

but as leading to a mention of the golden-crested kinglet. He is the least of all our winter birds, and one of the most engaging. Emerson's "atom in full breath" and "scrap of valor" would apply to him even better than to the titmouse. He says little,—zee, zee, zee is nearly the limit of his vocabulary; but his lively demeanor and the grace and agility of his movements are in themselves an excellent language, speaking infallibly a contented mind. (It is a fact, on which I forbear to moralize, that birds seldom look unhappy except when they are idle.) His diminutive size attracts attention even from those who rarely notice such things. About the first of December, a year ago, I was told of a man who had shot a humming-bird only a few days before in the vicinity of Boston. Of course I expressed a polite surprise, and assured my informant that such a remarkable capture ought by all means to be put on record in "The Auk," as every ornithologist in the land would be interested in it. On this he called upon the lucky sportsman's brother, who happened to be standing by, to corroborate the story. Yes, the latter said, the fact was as had been stated. "But then," he continued, "the bird didn't have a long bill, like a humming-bird;" and when I suggested that perhaps its crown was yellow, bordered with black, he said, "Yes, yes; that's the bird, exactly." So easy are startling discoveries to an observer who has just the requisite amount of knowledge,—enough, and (especially) not too much!

The brown creeper is quite as industrious and good-humored as the kinglet, but he is less taking in his personal appearance and less romantic in his mode of life. The same may be said of our two black-and-white woodpeckers, the downy and the hairy; while their more showy but less hardy relative, the flicker, evidently feels the weather a burden. The creeper and these three woodpeckers are with us in limited numbers every winter; and in the season of 1881-82 we had an altogether unexpected visit from the red-headed woodpecker,—such a thing as had not been known for a long time, if ever. Where the birds came from, and what was the occasion of their journey, nobody could tell. They arrived early in the autumn, and went away, with the exception of a few stragglers, in the spring; and as far as I know have never been seen since. It is a great pity they did not like us well enough to come again; for they are wide-awake, entertaining creatures, and gorgeously attired. I used to watch them in the oak groves of some

Longwood estates, but it was not till our second or third interview that I discovered them to be the authors of a mystery over which I had been exercising my wits in vain, a tree-frog's note in winter! One of their amusements was to drum on the tin girdles of the shade trees; and meanwhile they themselves afforded a pastime to the gray squirrels, who were often to be seen creeping stealthily after them, as if they imagined that Melanerpes erythrocephalus might possibly be caught, if only he were hunted long enough. I laughed at them; but, after all, their amusing hallucination was nothing but the sportsman's instinct; and life would soon lose its charm for most of us, sportsmen or not, if we could no longer pursue the unattainable.

Probably my experience is not singular, but there are certain birds, well known to be more or less abundant in this neighborhood, which for some reason or other I have seldom, if ever, met. For example, of the multitude of pine finches which now and then overrun Eastern Massachusetts in winter I have never seen one, while on the other hand I was once lucky enough to come upon a few of the very much smaller number which pass the summer in Northern New Hampshire. This was in the White Mountain Notch, first on Mount Willard and then near the Crawford House, at which latter place they were feeding on the lawn and along the railway track as familiarly as the goldfinches.

The shore larks, too, are no doubt common near Boston for a part of every year; yet I found half a dozen five or six years ago in the marsh beside a Back Bay street, and have seen none since. One of these stood upon a pile of earth, singing to himself in an undertone, while the rest were feeding in the grass. Whether the singer was playing sentinel, and sounded an alarm, I was not sure, but all at once the flock started off, as if on a single pair of wings.

Birds which elude the observer in this manner year after year only render themselves all the more interesting. They are like other species with which we deem ourselves well acquainted, but which suddenly appear in some quite unlooked-for time or place. The long-expected and the unexpected have both an especial charm. I have elsewhere avowed my favoritism for the white-throated sparrow; but I was never more delighted to see him than on one Christmas afternoon. I was walking in a back road, not far from the city, when I descried a sparrow ahead of me, feeding in the path, and, coming nearer, recognized my friend the white-throat. He held his ground till the last moment (time was precious to him that short day), and then flew into a bush to let me pass, which I had no sooner done than he was back again; and on my return the same thing was repeated. Far and near the ground was white, but just at this place the snow-plough had scraped bare a few square feet of earth, and by great good fortune this solitary and hungry straggler had hit upon it. I wondered what he would do when the resources of this garden patch were exhausted, but consoled myself with thinking that by this time he must be well used to living by his wits, and would probably find a way to do so even in his present untoward circumstances.

The snow-birds (not to be confounded with the snow buntings) should have at least a mention in such a paper as this. They are among the most familiar and constant of our winter guests, although very much less numerous at that time than in spring and autumn, when the fields and lanes are fairly alive with them.

A kind word must be said for the shrike, also, who during the three coldest months is to be seen on the Common oftener than any other of our native birds. There, at all events, he is doing a good work. May he live to finish it!

The blue jay stands by us, of course. You will not go far without hearing his scream, and catching at least a distant view of his splendid coat, which he is too consistent a dandy to put off for one of a duller shade, let the season shift as it will. He is not always good-natured; but none the less he is generally in good spirits (he seems to enjoy his bad temper), and, all in all, is not to be lightly esteemed in a time when bright feathers are scarce.

As for the jay's sable relatives, they are the most conspicuous birds in the winter landscape. You may possibly walk to Brookline and back without hearing a chickadee, or a blue jay, or even a goldfinch; but you will never miss sight and sound of the crows. Black against white is a contrast hard to be concealed. Sometimes they are feeding in the street, sometimes stalking about the marshes; but oftenest they are on the ice in the river, near the water's edge. For they know the use of friends, although they have never heard of Lord Bacon's "last fruit of friendship," and would hardly understand what that provident philosopher meant by saying that "the best way to represent to life the manifold use of friendship is to cast and see how many things there are which a man cannot do himself." How aptly their case illustrates the not unusual coexistence of formal ignorance with real knowledge! Having their Southern brother's fondness for fish without his skill in catching it, they adopt a plan worthy of the great essayist himself,—they court the society of the gulls; and with a temper eminently philosophical, not to say Baconian, they cheerfully sit at their patrons' second table. From the Common you may see them almost any day (in some seasons, at least) flying back and forth between the river and the harbor. One morning in early March I witnessed quite a procession, one small company after another, the largest numbering eleven birds, though it was nothing to compare with what seems to be a daily occurrence at some places further south. At another time, in the middle of January, I saw what appeared to be a flock of herring gulls sailing over the city, making progress in their own wonderfully beautiful manner, circle after circle. But I noticed that about a dozen of them were black! What were these? If they could have held their peace I might have gone home puzzled; but the crow is in one respect a very polite bird: he will seldom fly over your head without letting fall the compliments of the morning, and a vigorous caw, caw soon proclaimed my black gulls to be simply erratic specimens of Corvus Americanus. Why were they conducting thus strangely? Had they become so attached to their friends as to have taken to imitating them unconsciously? Or were they practicing upon the vanity of these useful allies of theirs, these master fishermen? Who can answer? The ways of shrewd people are hard to understand; and in all New England there is no shrewder Yankee than the crow.

A BIRD-LOVER'S APRIL

There shall be
Beautiful things made new, for the surprise
Of the sky-children.

— Keats.

Everywhere the blue sky belongs to them, and is their appointed rest, and their native country and their own natural homes, which they enter unannounced, as lords that are certainly expected, and yet these is a silent joy at their arrival.

— Coleridge.

A BIRD-LOVER'S APRIL.

It began on the 29th of March; in the afternoon of which day, despite the authority of the almanac and the banter of my acquaintances (March was March to them, and it was nothing more), I shook off the city's dust from my feet, and went into summer quarters. The roads were comparatively dry; the snow was entirely gone, except a patch or two in the shadow of thick pines under the northerly side of a hill; and all tokens seemed to promise an early spring. So much I learned before the hastening twilight cut short my first brief turn out-of-doors. In the morning would be time enough to discover what birds had already reported themselves at my station.

Unknown to me, however, our national weather bureau had announced a snow-storm, and in the morning I drew aside the curtains to look out upon a world all in white, with a cold, high wind blowing and snow falling fast. "The worst Sunday of the winter," the natives said. The "summer boarder" went to church, of course. To have done otherwise might have been taken for a confession of weakness; as if inclemency of this sort were more than he had bargained for. The villagers, lacking any such spur to right conduct, for the most part stayed at home; feeling it not unpleasant, I dare say, some of them, to have a natural inclination providentially confirmed, even at the cost of an hour's exercise with the shovel. The bravest parishioner of all, and the sweetest singer,—the song sparrow by name,—was not in the meeting-house, but by the roadside. What if the wind did blow, and the mercury stand at fifteen or twenty degrees below the freezing point? In cold as in heat "the mind is its own place."

Three days after this came a second storm, one of the heaviest snow-falls of the year. The robins were reduced to picking up seeds in the asparagus bed. The bluebirds appeared to be trying to glean something from the bark of trees, clinging rather awkwardly to the trunk meanwhile. (They are given to this, more or less, at all times, and it possibly has some connection with their half-woodpeckerish habit of nestling in holes.) Some of the snow-birds were doing likewise; I noticed one traveling up a trunk,—which inclined a good deal, to be sure,—exploring the crannies right and left, like any creeper. Half a dozen or more phœbes were in the edge of a wood; and they too seemed to have found out that, if worst came to worst, the tree-boles would yield a pittance for their relief. They often hovered against them, pecking hastily at the bark, and one at least was struggling for a foothold on the perpendicular surface. Most of the time, however, they went skimming over the snow and the brook, in the regular flycatcher style. The chickadees were put to little or no inconvenience, since what was a desperate makeshift to the others was to them only an every-day affair. It would take a long storm to bury their granary.[22] After the titmice, the fox-colored sparrows had perhaps the best of it. Looking out places where the snow had collected least, at the foot of a tree or on the edge of water, these adepts at scratching speedily turned up earth enough to checker the white with very considerable patches of brown. While walking I continually disturbed song sparrows, fox sparrows, tree sparrows, and snow-birds feeding in the road; and when I sat in my room I was advised of the approach of carriages by seeing these "pensioners upon the traveler's track" scurry past the window in advance of them.

It is pleasant to observe how naturally birds flock together in hard times,—precisely as men do, and doubtless for similar reasons. The

22. In the titmouse's cosmological system trees occupy a highly important place, we may be sure; while the purpose of their tall, upright method of growth no doubt receives a very simple and logical (and correspondingly lucid) explanation.

edge of the wood, just mentioned, was populous with them: robins, bluebirds, chickadees, fox sparrows, snow-birds, song sparrows, tree sparrows, phœbes, a golden-winged woodpecker, and a rusty blackbird. The last, noticeable for his conspicuous light-colored eye-ring, had somehow become separated from his fellows, and remained for several days about this spot entirely alone. I liked to watch his aquatic performances; they might almost have been those of the American dipper himself, I thought. He made nothing of putting his head and neck clean under water, like a duck, and sometimes waded the brook when the current was so strong that he was compelled every now and then to stop and brace himself against it, lest he should be carried off his feet.

It is clear that birds, sharing the frailty of some who are better than many sparrows, are often wanting in patience. As spring draws near they cannot wait for its coming. What it has been the fashion to call their unerring instinct is after all infallible only as a certain great public functionary is,—in theory; and their mistaken haste is too frequently nothing but a hurrying to their death. But I saw no evidence that this particular storm was attended with any fatal consequences. The snow completely disappeared within a day or two; and even while it lasted the song sparrows, fox sparrows, and linnets could be heard singing with all cheerfulness. On the coldest day, when the mercury settled to within twelve degrees of zero, I observed that the song sparrows, as they fed in the road, had a trick of crouching till their feathers all but touched the ground, so protecting their legs against the biting wind.

The first indications of mating were noticed on the 5th, the parties being two pairs of bluebirds. One of the females was rebuffing her suitor rather petulantly, but when he flew away she lost no time in following. Shall I be accused of slander if I suggest that possibly her No meant nothing worse than Ask me again? I trust not; she was only a bluebird, remember. Three days later I came upon two couples engaged in house-hunting. In this business the female takes the lead, with a silent, abstracted air, as if the matter were one of absorbing interest; while her mate follows her about somewhat impatiently, and with a good deal of talk, which is plainly intended to hasten the decision. "Come, come," he says; "the season is short, and we can't waste the whole of it in getting ready." I never could discover that his eloquence produced much effect, however. Her ladyship will have her own way; as indeed she ought to have, good soul, considering that she is to have the discomfort and the hazard. In one case I was puzzled by the fact that there seemed to be two females to one of the opposite sex. It really looked as if the fellow proposed to set up housekeeping with whichever should first find a house to her mind. But this is slander, and I hasten to take it back. No doubt I misinterpreted his behavior; for it is true—with sorrow I confess it—that I am as yet but imperfectly at home in the Sialian dialect.

For the first fortnight my note-book is full of the fox-colored sparrows. It was worth while to have come into the country ahead of time, as city people reckon, to get my fill of this Northern songster's music. Morning and night, wherever I walked, and even if I remained in-doors, I was certain to hear the loud and beautiful strain; to which I listened with the more attention because the birds, I knew, would soon be off for their native fields, beyond the boundaries of the United States.

It is astonishing how gloriously birds may sing, and yet pass unregarded. We read of nightingales and skylarks with a self-satisfied thrill of second-hand enthusiasm, and meanwhile our native songsters, even the best of them, are piping unheeded at our very doors. There may have been half a dozen of the town's people who noticed the presence of these fox sparrows, but I think it doubtful; and yet the birds, the largest, handsomest, and most musical of all our many sparrows, were, as I say, abundant everywhere, and in full voice.

One afternoon I stood still while a fox sparrow and a song sparrow sang alternately on either side of me, both exceptionally good vocalists, and each doing his best. The songs were of about equal length, and as far as theme was concerned were not a little alike; but the fox sparrow's tone was both louder and more mellow than the other's, while his notes were longer,—more sustained,—and his voice was "carried" from one pitch to another. On the whole, I had no hesitation about giving him the palm; but I am bound to say that his rival was a worthy competitor. In some respects, indeed, the latter was the more interesting singer of the two. His opening measure of three pips was succeeded by a trill of quite peculiar brilliancy and perfection; and when the other bird had ceased he suddenly took a lower perch, and began to rehearse an altogether different tune in a voice not more than half as loud as what he had been using; after which, as if to cap the climax, he several times followed the tune with a detached phrase or two in a still fainter voice. This last was pretty certainly an improvised cadenza, such a thing as I do not remember ever to have heard before from Melospiza melodia.

The song of the fox sparrow has at times an almost thrush-like quality; and the bird himself, as he flies up in front of you, might easily be mistaken for some member of that noble family. Once, indeed, when I saw him eating burning-bush berries in a Boston garden, I was half ready to believe that I had before my eyes a living example of the development of one species out of another,—a finch already well on his way to become a thrush. Most often, however, his voice puts me in mind of the cardinal grosbeak's; his voice, and perhaps still more his cadence, and especially his practice of the portamento.

The 11th of the month was sunny, and the next morning I came back from my accustomed rounds under a sense of bereavement: the fox sparrows were gone. Where yesterday there had been hundreds of them, now I could find only two silent stragglers. They had been well scattered over the township,—here a flock and there a flock; but in some way—I should be glad to have anybody tell me how—the word had passed from company to company that after sundown Friday night all hands would set out once more on their northward journey. There was one man, at least, who missed them, and in the comparative silence which followed their departure appreciated anew how much they had contributed to fill the wet and chilly April mornings with melody and good cheer.

The snow-birds tarried longer, but from this date became less and less abundant. For the first third of the month they had been as numerous, I calculated, as all other species put together. On one occasion I saw a large company of them chasing an albino, the latter dashing wildly round a pine-tree, with the whole flock in furious pursuit. They drove him off, across an impassable morass, before I could get close enough really to see him, but I presumed him to be of their own kind. As far as I could make out he was entirely white. For the moment it lasted, it was an exciting scene; and I was especially gratified to notice with what extreme heartiness and unanimity the birds discountenanced their wayward brother's heterodoxy. I agreed with them that one who cannot be content to dress like other people ought not to be allowed to live with them. The world is large,—let him go to Rhode Island!

On the evening of the 6th, just at dusk, I had started up the road for a lazy after-dinner saunter, when I was brought to a sudden halt by what on the instant I took for the cry of a night-hawk. But no night-hawk could be here thus early in the season, and listening further, I perceived that the bird, if bird it was, was on the ground, or, at any rate, not far from it. Then it flashed upon me that this was the note of the woodcock, which I had that very day startled upon this same hillside. Now, then, for another sight of his famous aerial courtship act! So, scrambling down the embankment, and clambering over the stone-wall, I pushed up the hill through bushes and briers, till, having come as near the bird as I dared, I crouched, and awaited further developments. I had not long to wait, for after a few yaks, at intervals of perhaps fifteen or twenty seconds, the fellow took to wing, and went soaring in a circle above me; calling hurriedly click, click, click, with a break now and then, as if for breath-taking. All this he repeated several times; but unfortunately it was too dark for me to see him, except as he crossed a narrow illuminated strip of sky just above the horizon line. I judged that he mounted to a very considerable height, and dropped invariably into the exact spot from which he had started. For a week or two I listened every night for a repetition of the yak; but I heard nothing more of it for a month. Then it came to my ears again, this time from a field between the road and a swamp. Watching my opportunity, while the bird was in the air, I hastened across the field, and stationed myself against a small cedar. He was still clicking high overhead, but soon alighted silently within twenty yards of where I was standing, and commenced to "bleat," prefacing each yak with a fainter syllable which I had never before been near enough to detect. Presently he started once more on his skyward journey. Up he went, in a large spiral, "higher still and higher" till the cedar cut off my view for an instant, after which I could not again get my eye upon him. Whether he saw me or not I cannot tell, but he dropped to the ground some rods away, and did not make another ascension, although he continued to call irregularly, and appeared to be walking about the field. Perhaps by this time the fair one for whose benefit all this parade was intended had come out of the swamp to meet and reward her admirer.

Hoping for a repetition of the same programme on the following night, I invited a friend from the city to witness it with me; one who, less fortunate than the "forest seer," had never "heard the woodcock's evening hymn," notwithstanding his knowledge of birds is a thousand-fold more than mine, as all students of American ornithology would unhesitatingly avouch were I to mention his name. We waited till dark; but though Philohela was there, and sounded his yak two or three times,—just enough to excite our hopes,—yet for some reason he kept to terra firma. Perhaps he was aware of our presence, and disdained to exhibit himself in the rôle of a wooer under our profane and curious gaze; or possibly, as my more scientific (and less sentimental) companion suggested, the light breeze may have been counted unfavorable for such high-flying exploits.

After all, our matter-of-fact world is surprisingly full of romance. Who would have expected to find this heavy-bodied, long-billed, gross-looking, bull-headed bird singing at heaven's gate? He a "scorner of the ground"? Verily, love worketh wonders! And perhaps it is really true that the outward semblance is sometimes deceptive. To be candid, however, I must end with confessing that, after listening to the woodcock's "hymn" a good many times, first and last, I cannot help thinking that it takes an imaginative ear to discover anything properly to be called a song in its monotonous click, click, even at its fastest and loudest.[23]

---

23. While this book is passing through the press (April 30th, 1885) I am privileged with another sight and sound of the woodcock's vespertine performance, and under peculiarly favorable conditions. In the account given above, sufficient distinction is not made between the clicking noise, heard while the bird is soaring, and the sounds which signalize his descent. The former is probably produced by the wings, although I have heretofore thought otherwise, while the latter are certainly vocal, and no doubt intended as a song. But they are little if at all louder than the click, click of the wings, and as far as I have ever been able to make out are nothing more than a series of quick, breathless whistles, with no attempt at either melody or rhythm.

    In the present instance I could see only the start and the "finish," when the bird several times passed directly by and over me, as I stood in a cluster of low birches, within two or three rods of his point of departure. His angle of flight was small; quite as if he had been going and coming from one field to another, in the ordinary course. Once I timed him, and found that he was on the wing for a few seconds more than a minute.

While I was enjoying the farewell matinée of the fox-colored sparrows on the 11th, suddenly there ran into the chorus the fine silver thread of the winter wren's tune. Here was pleasure unexpected. It is down in all the books, I believe, that this bird does not sing while on his travels; and certainly I had myself never known him to do anything of the sort before. But there is always something new under the sun.

"Who ever heard of th' Indian Peru?
Or who in venturous vessell measurèd
The Amazon's huge river, now found trew?
Or fruitfullest Virginia who did ever vew?"

I was all ear, of course, standing motionless while the delicious music came again and again out of a tangle of underbrush behind a dilapidated stone-wall,—a spot for all the world congenial to this tiny recluse, whose whole life, we may say, is one long game of hide-and-seek. Altogether the song was repeated twenty times at least, and to my thinking I had never heard it given with greater brilliancy and fervor. The darling little minstrel! he will never know how grateful I felt. I even forgave him when he sang thrice from a living bush, albeit in so doing he spoiled a sentence which I had already committed to "the permanency of print." Birds of all kinds will play such tricks upon us; but whether the fault be chargeable to fickleness or a mischievous spirit on their part, rather than to undue haste on the part of us their reporters, is a matter about which I am perhaps not sufficiently disinterested to judge. In this instance, however, it was reasonably certain that the singer did not show himself intentionally; for unless the whole tenor of his life belies him, the winter wren's motto is, Little birds should be heard, and not seen.

Two days afterward I was favored again in like manner. But not by the same bird, I think; unless my hearing was at fault (the singer was further off than before), this one's tune was in places somewhat broken and hesitating,—as if he were practicing a lesson not yet fully learned.

I felt under a double obligation to these two specimens of Anorthura troglodytes hiemalis: first for their music itself; and then for the support which it gave to a pet theory of mine, that all our singing birds will yet be found to sing more or less regularly in the course of the vernal migration.

Within another forty-eight hours this same theory received additional confirmation. I was standing under an apple-tree, watching a pair of titmice who were hollowing out a stub for a nest, when my ear caught a novel song not far away. Of course I made towards it; but the bird flew off, across the road and into the woods. My hour was up, and I reluctantly started homeward, but had gone only a few rods before the song was repeated. This was more than human nature could bear, and, turning back upon the run, I got into the woods just in time to see two birds chasing each other round a tree, both uttering the very notes which had so roused my curiosity. Then away they went; but as I was again bewailing my evil luck, one of them returned, and flew into the oak, directly over my head, and as he did so fell to calling anew, Sue, suky, suky. A single glance upward revealed that this was another of the silent migrants,—a brown creeper! Only once before had I heard from him anything beside his customary lisping zee, zee; and even on that occasion (in June and in New Hampshire) the song bore no resemblance to his present effort. I have written it down as it sounded at the moment, Sue, suky, suky, five notes, the first longer than the others, and all of them brusque, loud, and musical, though with something of a warbler quality.[24]

It surprised me to find how the migratory movement lagged for the first half of the month. A pair of white-breasted swallows flew over my head while I was attending to the winter wren on the 11th, and on the 14th appeared the first pine-creeping warblers,—welcome for their own sakes, and doubly so as the forerunners of a numerous and

---

24. Still further to corroborate my "pet theory," I may say here in a foot-note, what I have said elsewhere with more detail, that before the end of the following month the hermit thrushes, the olive-backed thrushes, and the gray-cheeked thrushes all sang for me in my Melrose woods.

    Let me explain, also, that when I call the brown creeper a silent migrant I am not unaware that others beside myself, and more than myself, have heard him sing while traveling. Mr. William Brewster, as quoted by Dr. Brewer in the History of North American Birds, has been exceptionally fortunate in this regard. But my expression is correct as far as the rule is concerned; and the latest word upon the subject which has come under my eye is this from Mr. E. P. Bicknell's "Study of the Singing of our Birds," in The Auk for April, 1884: "Some feeble notes, suggestive of those of Regulus satrapa, are this bird's usual utterance during its visit. Its song I have never heard."

splendid company; but aside from these two, I saw no evidence that a single new species arrived at my station for the entire fortnight.

Robins sang sparingly from the beginning, and became perceptibly more musical on the 8th, with signs of mating and jealousy; but the real robin carnival did not open till the morning of the 14th. Then the change was wonderful. Some of the birds were flying this way and that, high in air, two or three together; others chased each other about nearer the ground; some were screaming, some hissing, and more singing. So sudden was the outbreak and so great the commotion that I was persuaded there must have been an arrival of females in the night.

I have heard it objected against these thrushes, whose extreme commonness renders them less highly esteemed than they would otherwise be, that they find their voices too early in the morning. But I am not myself prepared to second the criticism. They are not often at their matins, I think, until the eastern sky begins to flush, and it is not quite certain to my mind that they are wrong in assuming that daylight makes daytime. I have questioned before now whether our own custom of sitting up for five or six hours after sunset, and then lying abed two or three hours after sunrise, may not have come down to us from times when there were still people in the world who loved darkness rather than light, because their deeds were evil; and whether, after all, in this as in some other respects, we might not wisely take pattern of the fowls of the air.

Individually, the phœbes were almost as noisy as the robins, but of course their numbers were far less. They are models of perseverance. Were their voice equal to the nightingale's they could hardly be more assiduous and enthusiastic in its use. As a general thing they are content to repeat the simple Phœbe, Phœbe (there are moods in the experience of all of us, I hope, when the repetition of a name is by itself music sufficient), but it is not uncommon for this to be heightened to Phœbe, O Phœbe; and now and then you will hear some fellow calling excitedly, Phœbe, Phœbe-be-be-be-be,—a comical sort of stuttering, in which the difficulty is not in getting hold of the first syllable, but in letting go the last one. On the 15th I witnessed a certain other performance of theirs,—one that I had seen two or three times the season previous, and for which I had been on the lookout from the first day of the month. I heard a series of chips, which might have been the cries of a chicken, but which, it appeared, did proceed from a phœbe, who, as I looked up, was just in the act of quitting his perch on the ridge-pole of a barn. He rose for perhaps thirty feet, not spirally, but in a zigzag course,—like a horse climbing a hill with a heavy load,—all the time calling, chip, chip, chip. Then he went round and round in a small circle, with a kind of hovering action of the wings, vociferating hurriedly, Phœbe, Phœbe, Phœbe; after which he shot down into the top of a tree, and with a lively flirt of his tail took up again the same eloquent theme. During the next few weeks I several times found birds of this species similarly engaged. And it is worthy of remark that, of the four flycatchers which regularly pass the summer with us, three may be said to be, in the habit of singing in the air, while the fourth (the wood pewee) does the same thing, only with less frequency. It is curious, also, on the other hand, that not one of our eight common New England thrushes, as far as I have ever seen or heard, shows the least tendency toward any such state of lyrical exaltation. Yet the thrushes are song birds par excellence, while the phœbe, the least flycatcher, and the kingbird are not supposed to be able to sing at all. The latter have the soul of music in them, at any rate; and why should it not be true of birds, as it is of human poets and would-be poets, that sensibility and faculty are not always found together? Perhaps those who have nothing but the sensibility have, after all, the better half of the blessing.

The golden-winged woodpeckers shouted comparatively little before the middle of the month, and I heard nothing of their tender wick-a-wick until the 22d. After that they were noisy enough. With all their power of lungs, however, they not only are not singers; they do not aspire to be. They belong to the tribe of Jubal. Hearing somebody drumming on tin, I peeped over the wall, and saw one of these pigeon woodpeckers hammering an old tin pan lying in the middle of the pasture. Rather small sport, I thought, for so large a bird. But that was a matter of opinion, merely, and evidently the performer himself had no such scruples. He may even have considered that his ability to play on this instrument of the tinsmith's went far to put him on an equality with some who boast themselves the only tool-using animals. True, the pan was battered and rusty; but it was resonant, for all that, and day after day he pleased himself with beating reveille upon it. One morning I found him sitting in a tree, screaming lustily in response to another bird in an adjacent field. After a while, waxing ardent, he dropped to the ground, and, stationing himself before his drum, proceeded to answer each cry of his rival with a vigorous rubadub, varying the programme with an occasional halloo. How long this would have lasted there is no telling, but he caught sight of me, skulking behind a tree-trunk, and flew back to his lofty perch, where he was still shouting when I came away. It was observable that, even in his greatest excitement, he paused once in a while to dress his feathers. At first I was inclined to take this as betraying a want of earnestness; but further reflection led me to a different conclusion. For I imagine that the human lover, no matter how consuming his passion, is seldom carried so far beyond himself as not to be able to spare now and then a thought to the parting of his hair and the tie of his cravat.

Seeing the great delight which this woodpecker took in his precious tin pan, it seemed to me not at all improbable that he had selected his summer residence with a view to being near it, just as I had chosen mine for its convenience of access to the woods on the one hand, and to the city on the other. I shall watch with interest to see whether he returns to the same pasture another year.

A few field sparrows and chippers showed themselves punctually on the 15th; but they were only scouts, and the great body of their followers were more than a week behind them. I saw no bay-winged buntings until the 22d, although it is likely enough they had been here for some days before that. By a lucky chance, my very first bird was a peculiarly accomplished musician: he altered his tune at nearly every repetition of it, sang it sometimes loudly and then softly, and once in a while added cadenza-like phrases. It lost nothing by being heard on a bright, frosty morning, when the edges of the pools were filmed with ice.

Only three species of warblers appeared during the month: the pine-creeping warblers, already spoken of, who were trilling on the 14th; the yellow-rumped, who came on the 23d; and the yellow red-polls, who followed the next morning. The black-throated greens were mysteriously tardy, and the black-and-white creepers waited for May-day.

A single brown thrush was leading the chorus on the 29th. "A great singer," my note-book says: "not so altogether faultless as some, but with a large voice and style, adapted to a great part;" and then is added, "I thought this morning of Titiens, as I listened to him!"—a bit of impromptu musical criticism, which, under cover of the saving quotation marks may stand for what it is worth.

Not long after leaving him I ran upon two hermit thrushes (one had been seen on the 25th), flitting about the woods like ghosts. I whistled softly to the first, and he condescended to answer with a low chuck, after which I could get nothing more out of him. This demure taciturnity is very curious and characteristic, and to me very engaging. The fellow will neither skulk nor run, but hops upon some low branch, and looks at you,—behaving not a little as if you were the specimen and he the student! And in such a case, as far as I can see, the bird equally with the man has a right to his own point of view.

The hermits were not yet in tune; and without forgetting the fox-colored sparrows and the linnets, the song sparrows and the bay-wings, the winter wrens and the brown thrush, I am almost ready to declare that the best music of the month came from the smallest of all the month's birds, the ruby-crowned kinglets. Their spring season is always short with us, and unhappily it was this year shorter even than usual, my dates being April 23d and May 5th. But we must be thankful for a little, when the little is of such a quality. Once I descried two of them in the topmost branches of a clump of tall maples. For a long time they fed in silence; then they began to chase each other about through the trees, in graceful evolutions (I can imagine nothing more graceful), and soon one, and then the other, broke out into song. "'Infinite riches in a little room,'" my note-book says, again; and truly the song is marvelous,—a prolonged and varied warble, introduced and often broken into, with delightful effect, by a wrennish chatter. For fluency, smoothness, and ease, and especially for purity and sweetness of tone, I have never heard any bird-song that seemed to me more nearly perfect. If the dainty creature would bear confinement,—on which point I know nothing,—he would make an ideal parlor songster; for his voice, while round and full,—in contrast with the goldfinch's, for example,—is yet, even at its loudest, of a wonderful softness and delicacy. Nevertheless, I trust that nobody will ever cage him. Better far go out-of-doors, and drink in the exquisite sounds as they drop from the thick of some tall pine, while you catch now and then a glimpse of the tiny author, flitting busily from branch to branch, warbling at his work; or, as you may oftener do, look and listen to your heart's content, while he explores some low cedar or a cluster of roadside birches, too innocent and happy to heed your presence. So you will carry home not the song only, but "the river and sky."

But if the kinglets were individually the best singers, I must still confess that the goldfinches gave the best concert. It was on a sunny after noon,—the 27th,—and in a small grove of tall pitch-pines. How many birds there were I could form little estimate, but when fifteen flew away for a minute or two the chorus was not perceptibly diminished. All were singing, twittering, and calling together; some of them directly over my head, the rest scattered throughout the wood. No one voice predominated in the least; all sang softly, and with an indescribable tenderness and beauty. Any who do not know how sweet the goldfinch's note is may get some conception of the effect of such a concert if they will imagine fifty canaries thus engaged out-of-doors. I declared then that I had never heard anything so enchanting, and I am not certain even now that I was over-enthusiastic.

A pine-creeping warbler, I remember, broke in upon the choir two or three times with his loud, precise trill. Foolish bird! His is a pretty song by itself, but set in contrast with music so full of imagination and poetry, it sounded painfully abrupt and prosaic.

I discovered the first signs of nest-building on the 13th, while investigating the question of a bird's ambi-dexterity. It happened that I had just been watching a chickadee, as he picked chip after chip from a dead branch, and held them fast with one claw, while he broke them in pieces with his beak; and walking away, it occurred to me to ask whether or not he could probably use both feet equally well for such a purpose. Accordingly, seeing another go into an apple-tree, I drew near to take his testimony on that point. But when I came to look for him he was nowhere in sight, and pretty soon it appeared that he was at work in the end of an upright stub, which he had evidently but just begun to hollow out, as the tip of his tail still protruded over the edge. A bird-lover's curiosity can always adapt itself to circumstances, and in this case it was no hardship to postpone the settlement of my newly raised inquiry, while I observed the pretty labors of my little architect. These proved to be by no means inconsiderable, lasting nearly or quite three weeks. The birds were still bringing away chips on the 30th, when their cavity was about eleven inches deep; but it is to be said that, as far as I could find out, they never worked in the afternoon or on rainy days.

Their demeanor toward each other all this time was beautiful to see; no effusive display of affection, but every appearance of a perfect mutual understanding and contentment. And their treatment of me was no less appropriate and delightful,—a happy combination of freedom and dignified reserve. I took it for an extremely neat compliment to myself, as well as incontestable evidence of unusual powers of discrimination on their part.

On my second visit the female sounded a call as I approached the tree, and I looked to see her mate take some notice of it; but he kept straight on with what he was doing. Not long after she spoke again, however; and now it was amusing to see the fellow all at once stand still on the top of the stub, looking up and around, as much as to say, "What is it, my dear? I see nothing." Apparently it was nothing, and he went head first into the hole again. Pretty soon, while he was inside, I stepped up against the trunk. His mate continued silent, and after what seemed a long time he came out, flew to an adjacent twig, dropped his load, and returned. This he did over and over (the end of the stub was perhaps ten feet above my head), and once he let fall a beakful of chips plump in my face. They were light, and I did not resent the liberty.

Two mornings later I found him at his task again, toiling in good earnest. In and out he went, taking care to bring away the shavings at every trip, as before, and generally sounding a note or two (keeping the tally, perhaps) before he dropped them. For the fifteen minutes or so that I remained, his mate was perched in another branch of the same tree, not once shifting her position, and doing nothing whatever except to preen her feathers a little. She paid no attention to her husband, nor did he to her. It was a revelation to me that a chickadee could possibly sit still so long.

Eight days after this they were both at work, spelling each other, and then going off in company for a brief turn at feeding.

So far they had never manifested the least annoyance at my espionage; but the next morning, as I stood against the tree, one of them seemed slightly disturbed, and flew from twig to twig about my head, looking at me from all directions with his shining black eyes. The reconnoissance was satisfactory, however; everything went on as before, and several times the chips rattled down upon my stiff Derby hat. The hole was getting deep, it was plain; I could hear the little carpenter hammering at the bottom, and then scrambling up the walls on his way out. One of the pair brought a black tidbit from a pine near by, and offered it to the other as he emerged into daylight. He took it from her bill, said chit,—chickadese for thank you,—and hastened back into the mine.

Finally, on the 27th, after watching their operations a while from the ground, I swung myself into the tree, and took a seat with them. To my delight, the work proceeded without interruption. Neither bird made any outcry, although one of them hopped round me, just out of reach, with evident curiosity. He must have thought me a queer specimen. When I drew my overcoat up after me and put it on, they flew away; but within a minute or two they were both back again, working as merrily as ever, and taking no pains not to litter me with their rubbish. Once the female (I took it to be she from her smaller size, not from this piece of shiftlessness) dropped her load without quitting the stub, a thing I had not seen either of them do before. Twice one brought the other something to eat. At last the male took another turn at investigating my character, and it began to look as if he would end with alighting on my hat. This time, too, I am proud to say, the verdict was favorable.

Their confidence was not misplaced, and unless all signs failed they reared a full brood of tits. May their tribe increase! Of birds so innocent and unobtrusive, so graceful, so merry-hearted, and so musical, the world can never have too many.

AN OWL'S HEAD HOLIDAY.

Let Euclid rest, and Archimedes pause,

And what the Swede intends, and what the French.

— Milton.

AN OWL'S HEAD HOLIDAY.

My trip to Lake Memphremagog was by the way, and was not expected to detain me for more than twenty-four hours; but when I went ashore at the Owl's Head Mountain-House, and saw what a lodge in the wilderness it was, I said to myself, Go to, this is the place; Mount Mansfield will stand for another year at least, and I will waste no more of my precious fortnight amid dust and cinders. Here were to be enjoyed many of the comforts of civilization, with something of the wildness and freedom of a camp. Out of one of the windows of my large, well-furnished room I could throw a stone into the trackless forest, where, any time I chose, I could make the most of a laborious half-hour in traveling half a mile. The other two opened upon a piazza; whence the lake was to be seen stretching away northward for ten or fifteen miles, with Mount Orford and his supporting hills in the near background; while I had only to walk the length of the piazza to look round the corner of the house at Owl's Head itself, at whose base we were. The hotel had less than a dozen guests and no piano, and there was neither carriage-road nor railway within sight or hearing. Yes, this was the place where I would spend the eight days which yet remained to me of idle time.

Of the eight days five were what are called unpleasant; but the unseasonable cold, which drove the stayers in the house to huddle about the fire, struck the mosquitoes with a torpor which made strolling in the woods a double luxury; while the rain was chiefly of the showery sort, such as a rubber coat and old clothes render comparatively harmless. Not that I failed to take a hand with my associates in grumbling about the weather. Table-talk would speedily come to an end in such circumstances if people were forbidden to criticise the order of nature; and it is not for me to boast any peculiar sanctity in this respect. But when all was over, it had to be acknowledged that I, for one, had been kept in-doors very little. In fact, if the whole truth were told, it would probably appear that my fellow boarders, seeing my persistency in disregarding the inclemency of the elements, soon came to look upon me as decidedly odd, though perhaps not absolutely demented. At any rate, I was rather glad than otherwise to think so. In those long days there must often have been a dearth of topics for profitable conversation, no matter how outrageous the weather, and it was a pleasure to believe that this little idiosyncracy of mine might answer to fill here and there a gap. For what generous person does not rejoice to feel that even in his absence he may be doing something for the comfort and well-being of his brothers and sisters? As Seneca said, "Man is born for mutual assistance."

According to Osgood's "New England," the summit of Owl's Head is 2,743 feet above the level of the lake, and the path to it is a mile and a half and thirty rods in length. It may seem niggardly not to throw off the last petty fraction; and indeed we might well enough let it pass if it were at the beginning of the route,—if the path, that is, were thirty rods and a mile and a half long. But this, it will be observed, is not the case; and it is a fact perfectly well attested, though perhaps not yet scientifically accounted for (many things are known to be true which for the present cannot be mathematically demonstrated), that near the top of a mountain thirty rods are equivalent to a good deal more than four hundred and ninety-five feet. Let the guide-book's specification stand, therefore, in all its surveyor-like exactness. After making the climb four times in the course of eight days, I am not disposed to abate so much as a jot from the official figures. Rather than do that I would pin my faith to an unprofessional-looking sign-board in the rear of the hotel, on which the legend runs, "Summit of Owl's Head 2¼ miles." For aught I know, indeed (in such a world as this, uncertainty is a principal mark of intelligence),—for aught I know, both measurements may be correct; which fact, if once it were established, would easily and naturally explain how it came to pass that I myself found the distance so much greater on some days than on others; although, for that matter, which of the two would be actually longer, a path which should rise

2,743 feet in a mile and a half, or one that should cover two miles and a quarter in reaching the same elevation, is a question to which different pedestrians would likely enough return contradictory answers.[25]

Yet let me not be thought to magnify so small a feat as the ascent of Owl's Head, a mountain which the ladies of the Appalachian Club may be presumed to look upon as hardly better than a hillock. The guide-book's "thirty rods" have betrayed me into saying more than I intended. It would have been enough had I mentioned that the way is in many places steep, while at the time of my visit the constant rains kept it in a muddy, treacherous condition. I remember still the undignified and uncomfortable celerity with which, on one occasion, I took my seat in what was little better than the rocky bed of a brook, such a place as I should by no means have selected for the purpose had I been granted even a single moment for deliberation.

"Hills draw like heaven" (as applied to some of us, it may be feared that this is rather an under-statement), and it could not have been more than fifteen minutes after I landed from the Lady of the Lake—the "Old Lady," as one of the fishermen irreverently called her—before I was on my way to the summit.

I was delighted then, as I was afterwards, whenever I entered the woods, with the extraordinary profusion and variety of the ferns. Among the rest, and one of the most abundant, was the beautiful Cystopteris bulbifera; its long, narrow, pale green, delicately cut, Dicksonia-like fronds bending toward the ground at the tip, as if about to take root for a new start, in the walking-fern's manner. Some of these could not have been less than four feet in length (including the stipe), and I picked one which measured about two feet and a half, and bore twenty-five bulblets underneath. Half a mile from the start, or thereabouts, the path skirts what I should call the fernery; a circular space, perhaps one hundred and fifty feet in diameter, set in the midst of the primeval forest, but itself containing no tree or shrub of any sort,—nothing but one dense mass of ferns. In the centre was a patch of the sensitive fern (Onoclea sensibilis), while around this, and filling nearly the entire circle, was a

25. The guide-book allows two hours for the mile and a half on Owl's Head, while it gives only an hour and a half for the three miles up Mount Clinton—from the Crawford House.

magnificent thicket of the ostrich fern (Onoclea struthiopteris), with sensibilis growing hidden and scattered underneath. About the edge were various other species, notably Aspidium Goldianum, which I here found for the first time, and Aspidium aculeatum, var. Braunii. All in all, it was a curious and pretty sight,—this tiny tarn filled with ferns instead of water,—one worth going a good distance to see, and sure to attract the notice of the least observant traveler.[26]

---

26. To bear out what has been said in the text concerning the abundance of ferns at Owl's Head, I subjoin a list of the species observed; premising that the first interest of my trip was not botanical, and that I explored but a very small section of the woods:—

    Polypodium vulgare.

    Adiantum pedatum.

    Pteris aquilina.

    Asplenium Trichomanes.

    A. thelypteroides.

    A. Filix-fœmina.

    Phegopteris polypodioides.

    P. Dryopteris.

    Aspidium marginale.

    A. spinulosum, variety undetermined.

    A. spinulosum, var. dilatatum.

    A. Goldianum.

    A. acrostichoides.

    A. aculeatum, var. Braunii.

    Cystopteris bulbifera.

    C. fragilis.

    Onoclea struthiopteris.

    O. sensibilis.

    Woodsia Ilvensis.

    Dicksonia punctilobula.

    Osmunda regalis.

    O. Claytoniana.

    O. cinnamomea.

    Botrychium lanceolatum.

    B. matricariæfolium.

    B. ternatum.

    B. Virginianum.

Ferns are mostly of a gregarious habit. Here at Owl's Head, for instance, might be seen in one place a rock thickly matted with the common polypody; in another a patch of the maiden-hair; in still another a plenty of the Christmas fern, or a smaller group of one of the beech ferns (Phegopteris polypodioides or Phegopteris Dryopteris). Our grape-ferns or moonworts, on the other hand, covet more elbow-room. The largest species (Botrychium Virginianum), although never growing in anything like a bed or tuft, was nevertheless common throughout the woods; you could gather a handful almost anywhere; but I found only one plant of Botrychium lanceolatum, and only two of Botrychium matricariæfolium (and these a long distance apart), even though, on account of their rarity and because I had never before seen the latter, I spent considerable time, first and last, in hunting for them. What can these diminutive hermits have ever done or suffered, that they should choose thus to live and die, each by itself, in the vast solitude of a mountain forest?

It was already the middle of July, so that I was too late for the better part of the wood flowers. The oxalis (Oxalis acetosella), or wood-sorrel was in bloom, however, carpeting the ground in many places. I plucked a blossom now and then to admire the loveliness of the white cup, with its fine purple lines and golden spots. If each had been painted on purpose for a queen, they could not have been more daintily touched. Yet here they were, opening by the thousand, with no human eye to look upon them. Quite as common (Wordsworth's expression, "Ground flowers in flocks," would have suited either) was the alpine enchanter's night-shade (Circæa alpina); a most frail and delicate thing, though it has little other beauty. Who would ever mistrust, to see it, that it would prove to be connected in any way with the flaunting willow-herb, or fire-weed? But such incongruities are not confined to the "vegetable kingdom." The wood-nettle was growing everywhere; a juicy-looking but coarse weed, resembling our common roadside nettles only in its blossoms. The cattle had found out what I never should have surmised,—having had a taste of its sting,—that it is good for food; there were great patches of it, as likewise of the pale touch-me-not (Impatiens pallida), which had been browsed over by them. It seemed to me that some of the ferns, the hay-scented for example, ought to have suited them better; but they passed these all by, as far as I could detect. About the edges of the woods, and in favorable positions well up the mountain-side, the flowering raspberry was flourishing; making no display of itself, but offering to any who should choose to turn aside and look at them a few blossoms such as, for beauty and fragrance, are worthy to be, as they really are, cousin to the rose. On one of my rambles I came upon some plants of a strangely slim and prim aspect; nothing but a straight, erect, military-looking, needle-like stalk, bearing a spike of pods at the top, and clasped at the middle by two small stemless leaves. By some occult means (perhaps their growing with Tiarella had something to do with the matter) I felt at once that these must be the mitrewort (Mitella diphylla). My prophetic soul was not always thus explicit and infallible, however. Other novelties I saw, about which I could make no such happy impromptu guess. And here the manual afforded little assistance; for it has not yet been found prac ticable to "analyze," and so to identify plants simply by the stem and foliage,—although I remember to have been told, to be sure, of a young lady who professed that at her college the instruction in botany was so thorough that it was possible for the student to name any plant in the world from seeing only a single leaf! But her college was not Harvard, and Professor Gray has probably never so much as heard of such an admirable method.

On the whole, it is good to have the curiosity piqued with here and there a vegetable stranger,—its name and even its family relationship a mystery. The leaf is nothing extraordinary, perhaps, yet who knows but that the bloom may be of the rarest beauty? Or the leaf is of a gracious shape and texture, but how shall we tell whether the flower will correspond with it? No; we must do with them as with chance acquaintances of our own kind. The man looks every inch a gentleman; his face alone seems a sufficient guaranty of good-breeding and intelligence; but none the less,—and not forgetting that charity thinketh no evil,—we shall do well to wait till we have heard him talk and seen how he will behave, before we put a final label upon him. Wait for the blossom and the fruit (the blossom is the fruit in its first stage); for the old rule is still the true one,—alike in botany and in morals,—"By their fruits ye shall know them."

What a world within a world the forest is! Under the trees were the shrubs,—knee-high rock-maples making the ground verdant for acres together, or dwarf thickets of yew, now bearing green acorn-like berries; while below these was a variegated carpet, oxalis and the flower of Linnæus, ferns and club-mosses (the glossy Lycopodium lucidulum was especially plentiful), to say nothing of the true mosses and the lichens.

Of all these things I should have seen more, no doubt, had not my head been so much of the time in the tree-tops. For yonder were the birds; and how could I be expected to notice what lay at my feet, while I was watching intently for a glimpse of the warbler that flitted from twig to twig amid the foliage of some beech or maple, the very lowest branch of which, likely enough, was fifty or sixty feet above the ground. It was in this way (so I choose to believe, at any rate) that I walked four or five times directly over the acute-leaved hepatica before I finally discovered it, notwithstanding it was one of the plants for which I had all the while been on the lookout.

I said that the birds were in the tree-tops; but of course there were exceptions. Here and there was a thrush, feeding on the ground; or an oven-bird might be seen picking his devious way through the underwoods, in paths of his own, and with a gait of studied and "sanctimonious" originality. In the list of the lowly must be put the winter wrens also; one need never look skyward for them. For a minute or two during my first ascent of Owl's Head I had lively hopes of finding one of their nests. Two or three of the birds were scolding earnestly right about my feet, as it were, and their cries redoubled, or so I imagined, when I approached a certain large, moss-grown stump. This I looked over carefully on all sides, putting my fingers into every possible hole and crevice, till it became evident that nothing was to be gained by further search. (What a long chapter we could write, any of us who are ornithologists, about the nests we did not find!) It dawned upon me a little later that I had been fooled; that it was not the nest which had been in question at all. That, wherever it was, had been forsaken some days before; and the birds were parents and young, the former distracting my attention by their outcries, while at the same moment they were ordering the youngsters to make off as quickly as possible, lest yonder hungry fiend should catch and devour them. If wrens ever laugh, this pair must have done so that evening, as they recalled to each other my eager fumbling of that innocent old stump. This opinion as to the meaning of their conduct was confirmed in the course of a few days, when I came upon another similar group. These were at first quite unaware of my presence; and a very pretty family picture they made, in their snuggery of overthrown trees, the father breaking out into a song once in a while, or helping his mate to feed the young, who were already able to pick up a good part of their own living. Before long, however, one of the pair caught sight of the intruder, and then all at once the scene changed. The old birds chattered and scolded, bobbing up and down in their own ridiculous manner (although, considered by itself, this gesture is perhaps no more laughable than some which other orators are applauded for making), and soon the place was silent and to all appearance deserted.

Notwithstanding Owl's Head is in Canada, the birds, as I soon found, were not such as characterize the "Canadian Fauna." Olive-backed thrushes, black-poll warblers, crossbills, pine linnets, and Canada jays, all of which I had myself seen in the White Mountains, were none of them here; but instead, to my surprise, were wood thrushes, scarlet tanagers, and wood pewees,—the two latter species in comparative abundance. My first wood thrush was seen for a moment only, and although he had given me a plain sight of his back, I concluded that my eyes must once more have played me false. But within a day or two, when half-way down the mountain path, I heard the well-known strain ringing through the woods. It was unquestionably that, and nothing else, for I sat down upon a convenient log and listened for ten minutes or more, while the singer ran through all those inimitable variations which infallibly distinguish the wood thrush's song from every other. And afterward, to make assurance doubly sure, I again saw the bird in the best possible position, and at short range. On looking into the subject, indeed, I learned that his being here was nothing wonderful; since, while it is true, as far as the sea-coast is concerned, that he seldom ventures north of Massachusetts, it is none the less down in the books that he does pass the summer in Lower Canada, reaching it, probably, by way of the valley of the St. Lawrence.

A few robins were about the hotel, and I saw a single veery in the woods, but the only members of the thrush family that were present in large numbers were the hermits. These sang everywhere and at all hours. On the summit, even at mid-day, I was invariably serenaded by them. In fact they seemed more abundant there than anywhere else; but they were often to be heard by the lake-side, and in our apple orchard, and once at least one of them sang at some length from a birch-tree within a few feet of the piazza, between it and the bowling alley. As far as I have ever been able to discover, the hermit, for all his name and consequent reputation, is less timorous and more approachable than any other New England representative of his "sub-genus."

On this trip I settled once more a question which I had already settled several times,—the question, namely, whether the wood thrush or the hermit is the better singer. This time my decision was in favor of the former. How the case would have turned had the conditions been reversed, had there been a hundred of the wood thrushes for one of the hermits, of course I cannot tell. So true is a certain old Latin proverb, that in matters of this sort it is impossible for a man to agree even with himself for any long time together.

The conspicuous birds, noticed by everybody, were a family of hawks. The visitor might have no appreciation of music; he might go up the mountain and down again without minding the thrushes or the wrens,—for there is nothing about the human ear more wonderful than its ability not to hear; but these hawks passed a good part of every day in screaming, and were bound to be attended to by all but the stone-deaf. A native of the region pointed out a ledge, on which, according to his account, they had made their nest for more than thirty years. "We call them mountain hawks," he said, in answer to an inquiry. The keepers of the hotel, naturally enough, called them eagles; while a young Canadian, who one day overtook me as I neared the summit, and spent an hour there in my company, pronounced them fish-hawks. I asked him, carelessly, how he could be sure of that, and he replied, after a little hesitation, "Why, they are all the time over the lake; and besides, they sometimes dive into the water and come up with a fish." The last item would have been good evidence, no doubt. My difficulty was that I had never seen them near the lake, and what was more conclusive, their heads were dark-colored, if not really black. A few minutes after this conversation I happened to have my glass upon one of them as he approached the mountain at some distance below us, when my comrade asked, "Looking at that bird?" "Yes," I answered; on which he continued, in a matter-of-fact tone, "That's a crow;" plainly thinking that, as I appeared to be slightly inquisitive about such matters, it would be a kindness to tell me a thing or two. I made bold to intimate that the bird had a barred tail, and must, I thought, be one of the hawks. He did not dispute the point; and, in truth, he was a modest and well-mannered young gentleman. I liked him in that he knew both how to converse and how to be silent; without which latter qualification, indeed, not even an angel would be a desirable mountain-top companion. He gave me information about the surrounding country such as I was very glad to get; and in the case of the hawks my advantage over him, if any, was mainly in this,—that my lack of knowledge partook somewhat more fully than his of the nature of Lord Bacon's "learned ignorance, that knows itself."

Whatever the birds may have been, "mountain hawks," "fish-hawks," or duck-hawks, their aerial evolutions, as seen from the summit, were beautiful beyond description. One day in particular three of them were performing together. For a time they chased each other this way and that at lightning speed, screaming wildly, though whether in sport or anger I could not determine. Then they floated majestically, high above us, while now and then one would set his wings and shoot down, down, till the precipitous side of the mountain hid him from view; only to reappear a minute afterward, soaring again, with no apparent effort, to his former height.

One of these noisy fellows served me an excellent turn. It was the last day of my visit, and I had just taken my farewell look at the enchanting prospect from the summit, when I heard the lisp of a brown creeper. This was the first of his kind that I had seen here, and I stopped immediately to watch him, in hopes he would sing. Creeper-like he tried one tree after another in quick succession, till at last, while he was exploring a dead spruce which had toppled half-way to the ground, a hawk screamed loudly overhead. Instantly the little creature flattened himself against the trunk, spreading his wings to their very utmost and ducking his head until, though I had been all the while eying his motions through a glass at the distance of only a few rods, it was almost impossible to believe that yonder tiny brown fleck upon the bark was really a bird and not a lichen. He remained in this posture for perhaps a minute, only putting up his head two or three times to peer cautiously round. Unless I misjudged him, he did not discriminate between the screech of the hawk and the ank, ank of a nuthatch, which followed it; and this, with an indefinable something in his manner, made me suspect him of being a young bird. Young or old, however, he had learned one lesson well, at all events, one which I hoped would keep him out of the talons of his enemies for long days to come.

It was pleasant to see how cheerfully he resumed work as soon as the alarm was over. This danger was escaped, at any rate; and why should he make himself miserable with worrying about the next? He had the true philosophy. We who pity the birds for their numberless perils are ourselves in no better case. Consumption, fevers, accidents, enemies of every name are continually lying in wait for our destruction. We walk surrounded with them; seeing them not, to be sure, but knowing, all the same, that they are there; yet feeling, too, like the birds, that in some way or other we shall elude them a while longer, and holding at second hand the truth which these humble creatures practice upon instinctively,—"Sufficient unto the day is the evil thereof."

Not far from this spot, on a previous occasion, I had very unexpectedly come face to face with another of the creeper's blood-thirsty persecutors. It happened that a warbler was singing in a lofty birch, and being in doubt about the song (which was a little like the Nashville's, but longer in each of its two parts and ending with a less confused flourish), I was of course very desirous to see the singer. But to catch sight of a small bird amid thick foliage, fifty feet or more above you, is not an easy matter, as I believe I have already once re marked. So when I grew weary of the attempt, I bethought myself to try the efficacy of an old device, well known to all collectors, and proceeded to imitate, as well as I could, the cries of some bird in distress. My warbler was imperturbable. He had no nest or young to be anxious about, and kept on singing. But pretty soon I was apprised of something in the air, coming toward me, and looking up, beheld a large owl who appeared to be dropping straight upon my head. He saw me in time to avoid such a catastrophe, however, and, describing a graceful curve, alighted on a low branch near by, and stared at me as only an owl can. Then away he went, while at the same instant a jay dashed into the thicket and out again, shouting derisively, "I saw you! I saw you!" Evidently the trick was a good one, and moderately well played; in further confirmation of which the owl hooted twice in response to some peculiarly happy efforts on my part, and then actually came back again for another look.

This proved sufficient, and he quickly disappeared; retiring to his leafy covert or hollow tree, to meditate, no doubt, on the strange creature whose unseasonable noises had disturbed his afternoon slumbers. Likely enough he could not readily fall asleep again for wondering how I could possibly find my way through the woods in the darkness of daylight. So difficult is it, we may suppose, for even an owl to put himself in another's place and see with another's eyes.

This little episode over, I turned again to the birch-tree, and fortunately the warbler's throat was of too fiery a color to remain long concealed; though it was at once a pleasure and an annoyance to find myself still unacquainted with at least one song out of the Blackburnian's repertory. In times past I had carefully attended to his music, and within only a few days, in the White Mountain Notch, I had taken note of two of its variations; but here was still another, which neither began with zillup, zillup, nor ended with zip, zip,—notes which I had come to look upon as the Blackburnian's sign-vocal. Yet it must have been my fault, not his, that I failed to recognize him; for every bird's voice has something characteristic about it, just as every human voice has tones and inflections which those who are sufficiently familiar with its owner will infallibly detect. The ear feels them, although words cannot describe them. Articulate speech is but a modern invention, as it were, in comparison with the five senses; and since practice makes perfect, it is natural enough that every one of the five should easily, and as a matter of course, perceive shades of difference so slight that lan guage, in its present rudimentary state, cannot begin to take account of them.

The other warblers at Owl's Head, as far as they came under my notice, were the black-and-white creeper, the blue yellow-backed warbler, the Nashville, the black-throated green, the black-throated blue, the yellow-rumped, the chestnut-sided, the oven-bird (already spoken of), the small-billed water thrush, the Maryland yellow-throat, the Canadian flycatcher, and the redstart.

The water thrush (I saw only one individual) was by the lake-side, and within a rod or two of the bowling alley. What a strange, composite creature he is! thrush, warbler, and sandpiper all in one; with such a bare-footed, bare-legged appearance, too, as if he must always be ready to wade; and such a Saint Vitus's dance! His must be a curious history. In particular, I should like to know the origin of his teetering habit, which seems to put him among the beach birds. Can it be that such frequenters of shallow water are rendered less conspicuous by this wave-like, up-and-down motion, and have actually adopted it as a means of defense, just as they and many more have taken on a color harmonizing with that of their ordinary surroundings?[27]

The black-throated blue warblers were common, and like most of their tribe were waiting upon offspring just out of the nest. I watched one as he offered his charge a rather large insect. The awkward fledgeling let it fall three times; and still the parent picked it up again, only chirping mildly, as if to say, "Come, come, my beauty, don't be quite so bungling." But even in the midst of their family cares, they still found leisure for music; and as they and the black-throated greens were often singing together, I had excellent opportunities to compare the songs of the two species. The voices, while both very peculiar, are at the same time so nearly alike that it was impossible for me on hearing the first note of either strain to tell whose it was. With the voice the similarity ends, however; for the organ does not make the singer, and while the blue seldom attempts more than a harsh, monotonous kree, kree, kree, the green possesses the true lyrical gift, so that few of our birds have a more engaging song than his simple Trees, trees, murmuring trees, or if you choose to understand it so, Sleep, sleep, pretty one, sleep.[28]

---

27. This bird (Siurus nævius) is remarkable for the promptness with which he sets out on his autumnal journey, appearing in Eastern Massachusetts early in August. Last year (1884) one was in my door-yard on the morning of the 7th. I heard his loud chip, and looking out of the window, saw him first on the ground and then in an ash-tree near a crowd of house sparrows. The latter were scolding at him with their usual cordiality, while he, on his part, seemed under some kind of fascination, returning again and again to walk as closely as he dared about the blustering crew. His curiosity was laughable. Evidently he thought, considering what an ado the sparrows were making, that something serious must be going on, something worth any bird's while to turn aside for a moment to look into. The innocent recluse! if he had lived where I do he would have grown used to such "windy congresses."

28. After all that has been said about the "pathetic fallacy," so called, it remains true that Nature speaks to us according to our mood. With all her "various language" she "cannot talk and find ears too." And so it happens that some, listening to the black-throated green warbler, have brought back a report of "Cheese, cheese, a little more cheese." Prosaic and hungry souls! This voice out of the pine-trees was not for them. They have caught the rhythm but missed the poetry.

I saw little of the blue yellow-backed warbler, but whenever I took the mountain path I was certain to hear his whimsical upward-running song, broken off at the end with a smart snap. He seemed to have chosen the neighborhood of the fernery for his peculiar haunt, a piece of good taste quite in accord with his general character. Nothing could well be more beautiful than this bird's plumage; and his nest, which is "globular, with an entrance on one side," is described as a wonder of elegance; while in grace of movement not even the titmouse can surpass him. Strange that such an exquisite should have so fantastic a song.

I have spoken of the rainy weather. There were times when the piazza was as far out-of-doors as it was expedient to venture. But even then I was not without excellent feathered society. Red-eyed vireos (one pair had their nest within twenty feet of the hotel), chippers, song sparrows, snow-birds, robins, waxwings, and phœbes were to be seen almost any moment, while the hermit thrushes, as I have before mentioned, paid us occasional visits. The most familiar of our door-yard friends, however, to my surprise, were the yellow-rumped warblers. Till now I had never found them at home except in the forests of the White Mountains; but here they were, playing the rôle which in Massachusetts we are accustomed to see taken by the summer yellow-birds, and by no others of the family. At first, knowing that this species was said to build in low evergreens, I looked suspiciously at some small spruces which lined the walk to the pier; but after a while I happened to see one of the birds flying into a rock-maple with something in his bill, and following him with my eye, beheld him alight on the edge of his nest. "About four feet from the ground," the book said (the latest book, too); but this lawless pair had chosen a position which could hardly be less than ten times that height,—considerably higher, at all events, than the eaves of the three-story house. It was out of reach in the small topmost branches, but I watched its owners at my leisure, as the maple was not more than two rods from my window. At this time the nestlings were nearly ready to fly, and in the course of a day or two I saw one of them sitting in a tree in the midst of a drenching rain. On my offering to lay hold of him he dropped into the grass, and when I picked him up both parents began to fly about me excitedly, with loud outcries. The male, especially, went nearly frantic, entering the bowling alley where I happened to be, and alighting on the floor; then, taking to the bole of a tree, he fluttered helplessly upon it, spreading his wings and tail, seeming to say as plainly as words could have done, "Look, you monster! here's another young bird that can't fly; why don't you come and catch him?" The acting was admirable,—all save the spreading of the tail; that was a false note, for the youngster in my hand had no tail feathers at all. I put the fellow upon a tree, whence he quickly flew to the ground (he could fly down but not up), and soon both parents were again supplying him with food. The poor thing had not eaten a morsel for possibly ten minutes, a very long fast for a bird of his age. I hoped he would fall into the hands of no worse enemy than myself, but the chances seemed against him. The first few days after quitting the nest must be full of perils for such helpless innocents.

For the credit of my own sex I was pleased to notice that it was the father-bird who manifested the deepest concern and the readiest wit, not to say the greatest courage; but I am obliged in candor to acknowledge that this feature of the case surprised me not a little.

In what language shall I speak of the song of these familiar myrtle warblers, so that my praise may correspond in some degree with the gracious and beautiful simplicity of the strain itself? For music to be heard constantly, right under one's window, it could scarcely be improved; sweet, brief, and remarkably unobtrusive, without sharpness or emphasis; a trill not altogether unlike the pine-creeping warbler's, but less matter-of-fact and business-like. I used to listen to it before I rose in the morning, and it was to be heard at intervals all day long. Occasionally it was given in an absent-minded, meditative way, in a kind of half-voice, as if the happy creature had no thought of what he was doing. Then it was at its best, but one needed to be near the singer.

In a clearing back of the hotel, but surrounded by the forest, were always a goodly company of birds, among the rest a family of yellow-bellied woodpeckers; and in a second similar place were white-throated sparrows, Maryland yellow-throats, and chestnut-sided warblers, the last two feeding their young. Immature warblers are a puzzling set. The birds themselves have no difficulty, I suppose; but seeing young and old together, and noting how unlike they are, I have before now been reminded of Launcelot Gobbo's saying, "It is a wise father that knows his own child."

While traversing the woods between these two clearings I saw, as I thought, a chimney swift fly out of the top of a tree which had been broken off at a height of twenty-five or thirty feet. I stopped, and pretty soon the thing was repeated; but even then I was not quick enough to be certain whether the bird really came from the stump or only out of the forest behind it. Accordingly, after sounding the trunk to make sure it was hollow, I sat down in a clump of raspberry bushes, where I should be sufficiently concealed, and awaited further developments. I waited and waited, while the mosquitoes, seeing how sheltered I was from the breeze, gathered about my head in swarms. A winter wren at my elbow struck up to sing, going over and over with his exquisite tune; and a scarlet tanager, also, not far off, did what he could—which was somewhat less than the wren's—to relieve the tedium of my situation. Finally, when my patience was well-nigh exhausted,—for the afternoon was wearing away and I had some distance to walk,—a swift flew past me from behind, and, with none of that poising over the entrance such as is commonly seen when a swift goes down a chimney, went straight into the trunk. In half a minute or less he reappeared without a sound, and was out of sight in a second. Then I picked up my rubber coat, and with a blessing on the wren and the tanager, and a malediction on the mosquitoes (so unjust does self-interest make us), started homeward.

Conservatives and radicals! Even the swifts, it seems, are divided into these two classes. "Hollow trees were good enough for our fathers; who are we that we should assume to know more than all the generations before us? To change is not of necessity to make progress. Let those who will, take up with smoky chimneys; for our part we prefer the old way."

Thus far the conservatives; but now comes the party of modern ideas. "All that is very well," say they. "Our ancestors were worthy folk enough; they did the best they could in their time. But the world moves, and wise birds will move with it. Why should we make a fetish out of some dead forefather's example? We are alive now. To refuse to take advantage of increased light and improved conditions may look like filial piety in the eyes of some: to us such conduct appears nothing better than a distrust of the Divine Providence, a subtle form of atheism. What are chimneys for, pray? And as for soot and smoke, we were made to live in them. Otherwise, let some of our opponents be kind enough to explain why we were created with black feathers."

So, in brief, the discussion runs; with the usual result, no doubt, that each side convinces itself.

We may assume, however, that these old-school and new-school swifts do not carry their disagreement so far as actually to refuse to hold fellowship with one another. Conscience is but imperfectly developed in birds, as yet, and they can hardly feel each other's sins and errors of belief (if indeed these things be two, and not one) quite so keenly as men are accustomed to do.

After all, it is something to be grateful for, this diversity of habit. We could not spare the swifts from our villages, and it would be too bad to lose them out of the Northern forests. May they live and thrive, both parties of them.

I am glad, also, for the obscurity which attends their annual coming and going. Whether they hibernate or migrate, the secret is their own; and for my part, I wish them the wit to keep it. In this age, when the world is in such danger of becoming omniscient before the time, it is good to have here and there a mystery in reserve. Though it be only a little one, we may well cherish it as a treasure.

A MONTH'S MUSIC

And now 'twas like all instruments,
Now like a lonely flute;
And now it is an angel's song,
That makes the heavens be mute.

— Coleridge.

A MONTH'S MUSIC.

The morning of May-day was bright and spring-like, and should have been signalized, it seemed to me, by the advent of a goodly number of birds; but the only new-comer to be found was a single black-and-white creeper. Glad as I was to see this lowly acquaintance back again after his seven months' absence, and natural as he looked on the edge of Warbler Swamp, bobbing along the branches in his own unique, end-for-end fashion, there was no resisting a sensation of disappointment. Why could not the wood thrush have been punctual? He would have made the woods ring with an ode worthy of the festival. Possibly the hermits—who had been with us for several days in silence—divined my thoughts. At all events, one of them presently broke into a song—the first Hylocichla note of the year. Never was voice more beautiful. Like the poet's dream, it "left my after-morn content."

It is too much to be expected that the wood thrush should hold himself bound to appear at a given point on a fixed date. How can we know the multitude of reasons, any one of which may detain him for twenty-four hours, or even for a week? It is enough for us to be assured, in general, that the first ten days of the month will bring this master of the choir. The present season he arrived on the 6th—the veery with him; last year he was absent until the 8th; while on the two years preceding he assisted at the observance of May-day.

All in all, I must esteem this thrush our greatest singer; although the hermit might dispute the palm, perhaps, but that he is merely a semi-annual visitor in most parts of Massachusetts. If perfection be held to consist in the absence of flaw, the hermit's is unquestionably the more nearly perfect song of the two. Whatever he attempts is done beyond criticism; but his range and variety are far less than his rival's, and, for my part, I can forgive the latter if now and then he reaches after a note lying a little beyond his best voice, and withal is too commonly wanting in that absolute simplicity and ease which lend such an ineffable charm to the performance of the hermit and the veery. Shakespeare is not a faultless poet, but in the existing state of public opinion it will hardly do to set Gray above him.

In the course of the month about which I am now writing (May, 1884) I was favored with thrush music to a quite unwonted degree. With the exception of the varied thrush (a New-Englander by accident only) and the mocking-bird, there was not one of our Massachusetts representatives of the family who did not put me in his debt. The robin, the brown thrush, the cat-bird, the wood thrush, the veery, and even the hermit (what a magnificent sextette!)—so many I counted upon hearing, as a matter of course; but when to these were added the Arctic thrushes—the olive-backed and the gray-cheeked—I gladly confessed surprise. I had never heard either species before, south of the White Mountains; nor, as far as I then knew, had anybody else been more fortunate than myself. Yet the birds themselves were seemingly unaware of doing anything new or noteworthy. This was especially the case with the olive-backs; and after listening to them for three days in succession I began to suspect that they were doing nothing new,—that they had sung every spring in the same manner, only, in the midst of the grand May medley, my ears had somehow failed to take account of their contribution. Their fourth (and farewell) appearance was on the 23d, when they sang both morning and evening. At that time they were in a bit of swamp, among some tall birches, and as I caught the familiar and characteristic notes—a brief ascending spiral—I was almost ready to believe myself in some primeval New Hampshire forest; an illusion not a little aided by the frequent lisping of black-poll warblers, who chanced just then to be remarkably abundant.

It was on the same day, and within a short distance of the same spot, that the Alice thrushes, or gray-cheeks, were in song. Their music was repeated a good many times, but unhappily it ceased whenever I tried to get near the birds. Then, as always, it put me in mind of the veery's effort, notwithstanding a certain part of the strain was quite out of the veery's manner, and the whole was pitched in decidedly too high a key. It seemed, also, as if what I heard could not be the complete song; but I had been troubled with the same feeling on previous occasions, and a friend whose opportunities have been better than mine reports a similiar experience; so that it is perhaps not uncharitable to conclude that the song, even at its best, is more or less broken and amorphous.

In their Northern homes these gray-cheeks are excessively wild and unapproachable; but while traveling they are little if at all worse than their congeners in this respect,—taking short flights when disturbed, and often doing nothing more than to hop upon some low perch to reconnoitre the intruder.

At the risk of being thought to reflect upon the acuteness of more competent observers, I am free to express my hope of hearing the music of both these noble visitors again another season. For it is noticeable how common such things tend to become when once they are discovered. An enthusiastic botanical collector told me that for years he searched far and near for the adder's-tongue fern, till one day he stumbled upon it in a place over which he had long been in the habit of passing. Marking the peculiarities of the spot he straightway wrote to a kindred spirit, whom he knew to have been engaged in the same hunt, suggesting that he would probably find the coveted plants in a particular section of the meadow back of his own house (in Concord); and sure enough, the next day's mail brought an envelope from his friend, inclosing specimens of Ophioglossum vulgatum, with the laconic but sufficient message, Eureka! There are few naturalists, I suspect, who could not narrate adventures of a like sort.

One such befell me during this same month, in connection with the wood wagtail, or golden-crowned thrush. Not many birds are more abundant than he in my neighborhood, and I fancied myself pretty well acquainted with his habits and manners. Above all, I had paid attention to his celebrated love-song, listening to it almost daily for several summers. Thus far it had invariably been given out in the afternoon, and on the wing. To my mind, indeed, this was by far its most interesting feature (for in itself the song is by no means of surpassing beauty), and I had even been careful to record the earliest hour at which

I had heard it—three o'clock P. M. But on the 6th of May aforesaid I detected a bird practicing this very tune in the morning, and from a perch! I set the fact down without hesitation as a wonder,—a purely exceptional occurrence, the repetition of which was not to be looked for. Anything might happen once. Only four days afterwards, however, at half-past six in the morning, I had stooped to gather some peculiarly bright-colored anemones (I can see the patch of rosy blossoms at this moment, although I am writing by a blazing fire while the snow is falling without), when my ear caught the same song again; and keeping my position, I soon descried the fellow stepping through the grass within ten yards of me, caroling as he walked. The hurried warble, with the common Weechee, weechee, weechee interjected in the midst, was reiterated perhaps a dozen times,—the full evening strain, but in a rather subdued tone. He was under no excitement, and appeared to be entirely by himself; in fact, when he had made about half the cir cuit round me he flew into a low bush and proceeded to dress his feathers listlessly. Probably what I had overheard was nothing more than a rehearsal. Within a week or two he would need to do his very best in winning the fair one of his choice, and for that supreme moment he had already put himself in training. The wise-hearted and obliging little beau! I must have been the veriest churl not to wish him his pick of all the feminine wagtails in the wood. As for the pink anemones, they had done me a double kindness, in requital for which I could only carry them to the city, where, in their modesty, they would have blushed to a downright crimson had they been conscious of one-half the admiration which their loveliness called forth.

Before the end of the month (it was on the morning of the 18th) I once more heard the wagtail's song from the ground. This time the affair was anything but a rehearsal. There were two birds,—a lover and his lass,—and the wooing waxed fast and furious. For that matter, it looked not so much like love-making as like an aggravated case of assault and battery. But, as I say, the male was warbling, and not improbably (so strange are the ways of the world), if he had been a whit less pugnacious in his addresses, his lady-love, who was plainly well able to take care of herself, would have thought him deficient in earnestness. At any rate, the wood wagtail is not the only bird whose courtship has the appearance of a scrimmage; and I believe there are still tribes of men among whom similar practices prevail, although the greater part of our race have learned, by this time, to take somewhat less literally the old proverb, "None but the brave deserve the fair." Love, it is true, is still recognized as one of the passions (in theory at least) even among the most highly civilized peoples; but the tendency is more and more to count it a tender passion.

While I am on the subject of marriage I may as well mention the white-eyed vireo. It had come to be the 16th of the month, and as yet I had neither seen nor heard anything of this obstreperous genius; so I made a special pilgrimage to a certain favorite haunt of his—Woodcock Swamp—to ascertain if he had arrived. After fifteen minutes or more of waiting I was beginning to believe him still absent, when he burst out suddenly with his loud and unmistakable Chip-a-weé-o. "Who are you, now?" the saucy fellow seemed to say, "Who are you, now?" Pretty soon a pair of the birds appeared near me, the male protesting his affection at a frantic rate, and the female repelling his advances with a snappish determination which might have driven a timid suitor desperate. He posed before her, puffing out his feathers, spreading his tail, and crying hysterically, Yip, yip, yaah,—the last note a downright whine or snarl, worthy of the cat-bird. Poor soul! he was well-nigh beside himself, and could not take no for an answer, even when the word was emphasized with an ugly dab of his beloved's beak. The pair shortly disappeared in the swamp, and I was not privileged to witness the upshot of the battle; but I consoled myself with believing that Phyllis knew how far she could prudently carry her resistance, and would have the discretion to yield before her adorer's heart was irremediably broken.

In this instance there was no misconceiving the meaning of the action; but whoever watches birds in the pairing season is often at his wit's end to know what to make of their demonstrations. One morning a linnet chased another past me down the road, flying at the very top of his speed, and singing as he flew; not, to be sure, the full and copious warble such as is heard when the bird hovers, but still a lively tune. I looked on in astonishment. It seemed incredible that any creature could sing while putting forth such tremendous muscular exertions; and yet, as if to show that this was a mere nothing to him, the finch had no sooner struck a perch than he broke forth again in his loudest and most spirited manner, and continued without a pause for two or three times the length of his longest ordinary efforts. "What lungs he must have!" I said to myself; and at once fell to wondering what could have stirred him up to such a pitch of excitement, and whether the bird he had been pursuing was male or female. He would have said, perhaps, if he had said anything, that that was none of my business.

What I have been remarking with regard to the proneness of newly discovered things to become all at once common was well illustrated for me about this time by these same linnets, or purple finches. One rainy morning, while making my accustomed rounds, enveloped in rubber, I stopped to notice a blue-headed vireo, who, as I soon perceived, was sitting lazily in the top of a locust-tree, looking rather disconsolate, and ejaculating with not more than half his customary voice and emphasis, Mary Ware!—Mary Ware! His indolence struck me as very surprising for a vireo; still I had no question about his identity (he sat between me and the sun) till I changed my position, when behold! the vireo was a linnet. A strange performance, indeed! What could have set this fluent vocalist to practicing exercises of such an inferior, disconnected, piecemeal sort? Within the next week or two, however, the same game was played upon me several times, and in different places. No doubt the trick is an old one, familiar to many observers, but to me it had all the charm of novelty.

There are no birds so conservative but that they will now and then indulge in some unexpected stroke of originality. Few are more artless and regular in their musical efforts than the pine warblers; yet I have seen one of these sitting at the tip of a tree, and repeating a trill which toward the close invariably declined by an interval of perhaps three tones. Even the chipping sparrow, whose lay is yet more monotonous and formal than the pine warbler's, is not absolutely confined to his score. I once heard him when his trill was divided into two portions, the concluding half being much higher than the other—unless my ear was at fault, exactly an octave higher. This singular refrain was given out six or eight times without the slightest alteration. Such freaks as these, however, are different from the linnet's Mary Ware, inasmuch as they are certainly the idiosyncrasies of single birds, not a part of the artistic proficiency of the species as a whole.

During this month I was lucky enough to close a little question which I had been holding open for a number of years concerning our very common and familiar black-throated green warbler. This species, as is well known, has two perfectly well-defined tunes of about equal length, entirely distinct from each other. My uncertainty had been as to whether the two are ever used by the same individual. I had listened a good many times, first and last, in hopes to settle the point, but hitherto without success. Now, however, a bird, while under my eye, delivered both songs, and then went on to give further proof of his versatility by repeating one of them minus the final note. This abbreviation, by the way, is not very infrequent with Dendrœca virens; and he has still another variation, which I hear once in a while every season, consisting of a grace note introduced in the middle of the measure, in such a connection as to form what in musical language is denominated a turn. At my first hearing of this I looked upon it as the private property of the bird to whom I was listening,—an improvement which he had accidentally hit upon. But it is clearly more than that; for besides hearing it in different seasons, I have noticed it in places a good distance apart. Perhaps, after the lapse of ten thousand years, more or less, the whole tribe of black-throated greens will have adopted it; and then, when some ornithologist chances to fall in with an old-fashioned specimen who still clings to the plain song as we now commonly hear it, he will fancy that to be the very latest modern improvement, and proceed forthwith to enlighten the scientific world with a description of the novelty.

Hardly any incident of the month interested me more than a discovery (I must call it such, although I am almost ashamed to allude to it at all) which I made about the black-capped titmouse. For several mornings in succession I was greeted on waking by the trisyllabic minor whistle of a chickadee, who piped again and again not far from my window. There could be little doubt about its being the bird that I knew to be excavating a building site in one of our apple-trees; but I was usually not out-of-doors until about five o'clock, by which time the music always came to an end. So one day I rose half an hour earlier than common on purpose to have a look at my little matutinal serenader. My conjecture proved correct. There sat the tit, within a few feet of his apple-branch door, throwing back his head in the truest lyrical fashion, and calling Hear, hear me, with only a breathing space between the repetitions of the phrase. He was as plainly singing, and as completely absorbed in his work, as any thrasher or hermit thrush could have been. Heretofore I had not realized that these whistled notes were so strictly a song, and as such set apart from all the rest of the chickadee's repertory of sweet sounds; and I was delighted to find my tiny pet recognizing thus unmistakably the difference between prose and poetry.

But we linger unduly with these lesser lights of song. After the music of the Alice and the Swainson thrushes, the chief distinction of May, 1884, as far as my Melrose woods were concerned, was the entirely unexpected advent of a colony of rose-breasted grosbeaks. For five seasons I had called these hunting-grounds my own, and during that time had seen perhaps about the same number of specimens of this royal species, always in the course of the vernal migration. The present year the first comer was observed on the 15th—solitary and, except for an occasional monosyllable, silent. Only one more straggler, I assumed. But on the following morning I saw four others, all of them males in full plumage, and two of them in song. To one of these I attended for some time. According to my notes "he sang beautifully, although not with any excitement, nor as if he were doing his best. The tone was purer and smoother than the robin's, more mellow and sympathetic, and the strain was especially characterized by a dropping to a fine contralto note at the end." The next day I saw nothing of my new friends till toward night. Then, after tea, I strolled into the chestnut grove, and walking along the path, noticed a robin singing freely, remarking the fact because this noisy bird had been rather quiet of late. Just as I passed under him, however, it flashed upon me that the voice and song were not exactly the robin's. They must be the rose-breast's then; and stepping back to look up, I beheld him in gorgeous attire, perched in the top of an oak. He sang and sang, while I stood quietly listening. Pretty soon he repeated the strain once or twice in a softer voice, and I glanced up instinctively to see if a female were with him; but instead, there were two males sitting within a yard of each other. They flew off after a little, and I resumed my saunter. A party of chimney swifts were shooting hither and thither over the trees, a single wood thrush was chanting not far away, and in another direction a tanager was rehearsing his chip-cherr with characteristic assiduity. Presently I began to be puzzled by a note which came now from this side, now from that, and sounded like the squeak of a pair of rusty shears. My first conjecture about the origin of this hic it would hardly serve my reputation to make public; but I was not long in finding out that it was the grosbeaks' own, and that, instead of three, there were at least twice that number of these brilliant strangers in the grove. Altogether, the half hour was one of very enjoyable excitement; and when, later in the evening, I sat down to my note-book, I started off abruptly in a hortatory vein,—"Always take another walk!"

In the morning, naturally enough, I again turned my steps toward the chestnut grove. The rose-breasts were still there, and one of them earned my thanks by singing on the wing, flying slowly—half-hovering, as it were—and singing the ordinary song, but more continuously than usual. That afternoon one of them was in tune at the same time with a robin, affording me the desired opportunity for a direct comparison. "It is really wonderful," my record says, "how nearly alike the two songs are; but the robin's tone is plainly inferior,—less mellow and full. In general, too, his strain is pitched higher; and, what perhaps is the most striking point of difference, it frequently ends with an attempt at a note which is a little out of reach, so that the voice breaks." (This last defect, by the bye, the robin shares with his cousin the wood thrush, as already remarked.) A few days afterwards, to confirm my own impression about the likeness of the two songs, I called the attention of a friend with whom I was walking, to a grosbeak's notes, and asked him what bird's they were. He, having a good ear for matters of this kind, looked somewhat dazed at such an inquiry, but answered promptly, "Why, a robin's, of course." As one day after another passed, however, and I listened to both species in full voice on every hand, I came to feel that I had overestimated the resemblance. With increasing familiarity I discerned more and more clearly the respects in which the songs differed, and each came to have to my ear an individuality strictly its own. They were alike, doubtless,—as the red-eyed vireo's and the blue-head's are,—and yet they were not alike. Of one thing I grew, better and better assured: the grosbeak is out of all comparison the finer musician of the two. To judge from my last-year's friends, however, his concert season is very short—the more's the pity.

I begin to perceive (indeed it has been dawning upon me for some time) that our essay is not to fulfill the promise of its caption. Instead of the glorious fullness and variety of the month's music (for May, in this latitude, is the musical month of months) the reader has been put off with a few of the more exceptional features of the carnival. He will overlook it, I trust; and as for the great body of the chorus, who have not been honored with so much as a mention, they, I am assured, are far too amiable to take offense at any such unintentional slight. Let me conclude, then, with transcribing from my note-book an evening entry or two. Music is never so sweet as at the twilight hour; and the extracts may serve at least as a convenient and quasi-artistic ending for a paper which, so to speak, has run away with its writer. The first is under date of the 19th:—

"Walked, after dinner, in the Old Road, as I have done often of late, and sat for a while at the entrance to Pyrola Grove. A wood thrush was singing not far off, and in the midst a Swainson thrush vouchsafed a few measures. I wished the latter would continue, but was thankful for the little. A tanager called excitedly, Chip-cherr, moving from tree to tree meanwhile, once to a birch in full sight, and then into the pine over my head. As it grew dark the crowd of warblers were still to be seen feeding busily, making the most of the lingering daylight. A small-billed water thrush was teetering along a willow-branch, while his congeners, the oven-birds, were practicing their aerial hymn. One of these went past me as I stood by the roadside, rising very gradually into the air and repeating all the way, Chip, chip, chip, chip, till at last he broke into the warble, which was a full half longer than usual. He was evidently doing his prettiest. No vireos sang after sunset. A Maryland yellow-throat piped once or twice (he is habitually an evening musician), and the black-throated greens were in tune, but the rest of the warblers were otherwise engaged. Finally, just as a distant whippoorwill began to call, a towhee sang once from the woods; and a moment later the stillness was broken by the sudden outburst of a thrasher. 'Now then,' he seemed to say, 'if the rest of you are quite done, I will see what I can do.' He kept on for two or three minutes in his best manner, and at the same time a pair of cat-birds were whispering love together in the thicket. Then an ill-timed carriage came rattling along the road, and when it had passed, every bird's voice was hushed. The hyla's tremulous cry was the only musical sound to be heard. As I started away, one of these tree-frogs hopped out of my path, and I picked him up at the second or third attempt. What did he think, I wonder, when I turned him on his back to look at the disks at his finger-tips? Probably he supposed that his hour was come; but I had no evil designs upon him,—he was not to be drowned in alcohol at present. Walking homeward I heard the robin's scream now and again; but the thrasher's was the last song, as it deserved to be."

Two days later I find the following:—

"Into the woods by the Old Road. As I approached them, a little after sundown, a chipper was trilling, and song sparrows and golden warblers were singing,—as were the black-throated greens also, and the Maryland yellow-throats. A wood thrush called brusquely, but offered no further salute to the god of day at his departure. Oven-birds were taking to wing on the right and left. Then, as it grew dark, it grew silent,—except for the hylas,—till suddenly a field sparrow gave out his sweet strain once. After that all was quiet for another interval, till a thrasher from the hillside began to sing. He ceased, and once more there was stillness. All at once the tanager broke forth in a strangely excited way, blurting out his phrase two or three times and subsiding as abruptly as he had commenced. Some crisis in his love-making, I imagined. Now the last oven-bird launched into the air and let fall a little shower of melody, and a whippoorwill took up his chant afar off. This should have been the end; but a robin across the meadow thought otherwise, and set at work as if determined to make a night of it. Mr. Early-and-late, the robin's name ought to be. As I left the wood the whippoorwill followed; coming nearer and nearer, till finally he overpassed me and sang with all his might (while I tried in vain to see him) from a tree or the wall, near the big buttonwood. He too is an early riser, only he rises before nightfall instead of before daylight."